HOPE
FOR
AMERICA

Valentine Publishing House
P.O. Box 27422
Denver, Colorado 80227

The Scripture quotations contained herein are from the *New Revised
Standard Version Bible,* copyright © 1989 by the Division of Christian
Education of the National Council of the Churches of Christ in the U.S.A.
Used by permission. All rights reserved.

Cover Graphics—Desert Isle Design LLC

Publisher's Cataloging-in-Publication Data

Christ-in-Congress Campaign.
Hope for America / 2016 Christ-in-Congress Campaign.

p. : ill. ; cm.

ISBN–10: 0-9796331-0-9
ISBN–13: 978-0-9796331-0-2

1. United States—politics and government—21st century. 2. United
States—economic conditions—21st century. 3. United States—social
conditions—21st century. I. Title.

JK275.R66 2012
320.60973—dc22

Printed in the United States of America.

"You know that the rulers of the Gentiles lord it over them, and their great ones are tyrants over them. It will not be so among you; but whoever wishes to be great among you must be your servant, and whoever wishes to be first among you must be your slave."

Matthew 20:25–27

TABLE OF CONTENTS

PART ONE

THE PROBLEM

CHAPTER ONE

HOW WILL WE PAY FOR THIS?

In an attempt to stimulate the economy, George W. Bush signed into law the Economic Stimulus Act of 2008. Under this program, most taxpayers received a $300 rebate check in the mail.[1] The goal of this program was for Americans to start spending money immediately.

Washington wanted taxpayers to make major financial decisions to keep the economy rolling. They wanted potential new-car buyers to visit their local Honda and Toyota dealerships, future homeowners were supposed to use the money for a down payment, and small-business owners were expected to open up additional retail locations and hire more employees.

What do you think the average citizen did with their $300 check? Did they run out and start shopping? Do you think the rich considered it some kind of joke, laughing as they deposited the funds in their bank accounts? Would an Economic Stimulus Act passed by Congress send a warning signal to the American people that something may be seriously wrong with our government, economy and financial system? If a big red flag had been created, do you think the typical American might pull back on his or her financial, investment and spending plans?

Because the $300 stimulus checks did not have the desired effect on the U.S. economy that Washington had hoped for, Congress took further action. According to an article by *The Wall Street Journal, President George W. Bush signed into law an unprecedented $700 billion plan to rescue the U.S. financial system, one of the largest-ever government interventions in the nation's economy—and almost certainly not the last.*[2]

Four months later on February 18, 2009, *President Barack Obama signed his $787 billion economic stimulus package into law with an upbeat speech emphasizing the road to recovery.* According to an article in *The Wall Street Journal, it was a remarkably speedy achievement, enacted into law less than a month after Mr. Obama took office.*[3]

If you divide the estimated 300 million people living in America into George W. Bush's $700 billion bailout, it would leave a debt in the amount of $2,333 for each citizen ($700,000,000,000 ÷ 300,000,000 = $2,333). This figure was doubled by President Obama's $787 billion stimulus package, and it would later be compounded by the interest necessary to finance the debt over several years.

Because it would not be appropriate to ask a new-born baby to pay back $5,000 to the United States Treasury, just as it would not be appropriate to ask a ninety-six-year-old lady living in a nursing home to pay back the debt, the responsibility for these actions would be forced upon every working-class head of household. For example, a family of five may have to pay back $25,000 (5 x $5,000 per citizen = $25,000). If the debt were financed over thirty years at 5 percent without any interest payments being made, the amount would increase to more than $110,000.

To make matters worse, on August 3, 2011, the federal government's borrowing limit was increased by $2.4 trillion. Almost immediately, President Obama devised a plan to spend part of the money on what he called "The American Jobs Act." According to an article in *The Washington Post* on September 8, 2011, *President Obama urged Congress Thursday night to pass a $447 billion plan that he said will get the economy moving and create jobs.*[4]

Several months later on December 27, 2011, President Obama wanted to ask Congress for more money. According to an article by Reuters, *The White House plans to ask Congress by the end of the week for an increase in the government's debt ceiling to allow the United States to pay its bills on time, according to a senior Treasury Department official on Tuesday. The debt limit currently stands at $15.194 trillion and would increase to $16.394 trillion with the request.*[5]

When we take the number of people living in America divided into a $16.5 trillion deficit, it comes to $55,000 per person ($16,500,000,000,000 ÷ 300,000,000 = $55,000). Because young schoolchildren do not have the ability to pay back this amount, the responsibility will fall upon every head of household. A hardworking, married factory worker with three young children could be required to pay the

U.S. Treasury $275,000 (5 x $55,000 per citizen = $275,000).

Because the average citizen has no desire to pay back this amount, the U.S. government will be forced to finance the debt. At a 5 percent interest rate, the factory worker would have to make $1,146 monthly payments just to cover the interest ($275,000 x .05 ÷ 12 = $1,146). When the average factory worker is struggling to make his monthly housing expense, how would it be possible to ask him to pay an additional $1,146 per month to cover the government's interest payments? If the factory worker failed to make the interest payments, his portion of the debt would increase to more than 1.2 million within thirty years.

If you were part of the 2016 Christ-in-Congress Campaign, how would you describe America's current financial situation?

CHAPTER TWO

VOTE FOR ME AND EVERYTHING WILL BE FREE

During the 2008 presidential campaign, there was a lot of media coverage about all the free benefits the American people would receive if only they voted for Candidate-A. Because everybody in America wanted to receive government benefits without having to pay for anything, Candidate-B also started making a lot of campaign promises.

One day when Candidate-A looked over the crowd, he was able to identify a man called "Joe Six-Pack." In an attempt to win Six-Pack's vote, Candidate-A said, *If you vote for me, I will give everybody in America a free six-pack of beer.* Because the crowd went wild upon hearing this great news, Candidate-B made an even better promise by saying, If you vote for me, I will give everybody in America a free *case* of beer, plus free health care insurance. Nobody will have to pay for health care anymore!

In an attempt to exceed this offer, Candidate-A said, If you vote for me, I will give everybody free beer, free health care insurance and a free car! We will call it the Cash-for-Clunkers program! The federal government will pay you to buy a new car! We will recycle your old gas-guzzling automobiles, and everybody can drive an environmentally friendly, fuel-efficient vehicle.

Now that the crowds were ecstatic, Candidate-B said, If you vote for me, I will give you free beer, free health care insurance, a free car and a free house! Nobody will have to make mortgage payments any longer. We will call it the Federal Home Loan Modification Program. The federal government will help millions of homeowners lower their interest rates and cut hundreds of thousands of dollars off their principal balance.

Because Candidate-A could not exceed this promise, Candidate-B won the election. After being elected to office, President Obama started fulfilling his campaign promises. According to an article published by CNN on October 29, 2009, *The Cash for Clunkers program gave car buyers rebates of up to $4,500 if they traded in less fuel-efficient vehicles for new vehicles that met certain fuel economy requirements.*[1]

A total of $3 billion was allotted for those rebates. But the overwhelming majority of sales would have taken place anyway at some time in the last half of 2009, according to Edmunds.com. That means the government ended up spending about $24,000 each for those 125,000 additional vehicle sales.[2]

If you are wondering how the federal government could spend $24,000 for each additional vehicle sold under the Cash for Clunkers program, a report published by the Department of Transportation describes the administration costs as follows:

Of the $1 billion budget, $50 million is allocated to cover government administrative costs. This includes the National Highway Traffic Safety Administration (NHTSA) costs for program development, website development, NHTSA enforcement hotline, formation of the dealer registration program (shared by NHTSA and dealers), formation of the salvage yard registration program (shared by NHTSA and salvage yards), enforcing penalties and final evaluation of the Act.[3]

In order to administer the Cash for Clunker program, the Department of Transportation needed to staff an entirely new division. According to program details, NHTSA wanted to hire thirty employees to create new dealership forms. They also wanted to hire 200 contractors for data entry and telephone support—all to implement a government-subsidized program for a very short period of time.

After spending $3 billion, Congress approved an additional $2 billion on July 31, 2009, to extend the Cash for Clunkers program a few more months. After spending $5 billion ($5,000,000,000), the Obama Administration was finally ready to implement the long-awaited Home Loan Modification Program.

According to an article published by CNN on April 16, 2009, *The Obama Administration's loan modification program is finally underway. The Treasury Department announced Wednesday the first six participants to sign up for President Obama's plan. They include three of the nation's largest banks: JPMorgan Chase, which will get up to $3.6 billion in subsidy and incentive payments; Wells Fargo, $2.9 billion; and Citigroup, $2 billion.*

The modification plan calls for the servicer to reduce interest rates so that the monthly obligation is no more than 38% of a borrower's pre-tax income, and then the government would kick in money to bring payments down to 31% of income. Servicers can also reduce the loan balance to achieve these affordability levels. The government will share in the cost, up to the amount the servicer would have received if it had reduced the interest rates.

In addition to subsidizing the interest rates, servicers will use the Treasury funding to pay for incentives for themselves, homeowners and investors. The program gives servicers $1,000 for each modification and another $1,000 a year for three years if the borrower stays current. It will also give $500 to servicers and $1,500 to mortgage holders if they modify at-risk loans before the borrower falls behind. Homeowners, meanwhile, will get up to $1,000 a year for five years if they keep up with payments.[4]

The Home Loan Modification Program may sound like a great way for homeowners to cash in on some free government money, but it has also enticed many Americans in good standing with their lenders to default on their commitments. By making these kinds of promises, the Obama Administration released a subconscious message to the American people saying, *If you default on your loan, the government will help you lower the payments; but if you don't default, then you will not receive any free benefits.* After releasing this message, hardworking Americans who were accustomed to paying their bills on time suddenly had an excuse to stop making their mortgage payments.

In addition to releasing a *welfare state* message to the American people, the fundamental problem behind the Obama Home Loan Modification Program is that lenders are not required to participate. Once a deed of trust has been signed, a mortgage company is under no obligation to reduce anyone's interest rates or principle balance. Once a borrower signs a deed of trust, they enter a legally binding agreement to make all their payments on time. In the event of a default, the lender has the right to foreclose on the property.

When a borrower defaults on their obligations, the lender (or the company servicing the lender's loans) has a right to file notice with the public trustee in the county where the property is located. After all the legal requirements have been fulfilled (depending on which state you live in), the property will be advertised for sale in the local newspaper under Legal Notices.

On the day of the sale, anyone can show up at the advertised location with certified funds to buy the property. If a lender is owed $200,000, the asset manager for the mortgage company may decide to take an $80,000 loss and offer the property to the general public for $120,000. Investors who attend these auctions on a regular basis may compete against each other, increasing their bids to $130,000. Once the highest bidder delivers certified funds to the public trustee, the sale is considered final after the redemption period is complete.

During this redemption period, the second or third lien holders can come forward to buy the investor's bid to protect their financial interests. In most cases, the second and third lien holders accept a loss. After the redemption period has expired, the public trustee will deliver a deed of trust to the investor.

At this point, the investor is considered the legal owner of the property, and the people living inside the house (the former owners) are considered by law no different than a tenant without a lease. To evict these people, all the investor needs to do is file an unlawful detainer case in small claims court. In the event the former owners do not vacate the property when notified, the investor can file a writ of restitution with the sheriff's office and schedule a time to move all the former owner's personal property to the public sidewalk.

The problem with the Obama Home Mortgage Modification Program is that mortgage companies have very little or no incentive and are under no obligation to lower anybody's interest rates, payment schedule or principal balance after a deed of trust has been signed. The Home Mortgage Modification Program only introduces third-party negotiators into an existing deal to shuffle around some government paperwork on the borrower's behalf.

In most cases, the foreclosure process moves along at a very fast pace while the third-party negotiators are attempting to reduce the homeowner's principal balance. In many situations, the property has already gone to public sale, while the unaware homeowners are waiting to hear some good news about lower payments. Unfortunately, many homeowners have put their trust in the federal government's promise, hoping to take advantage of a good deal, then unexpectedly find themselves being evicted from their homes.

A good example of how the Home Loan Modification Program has the ability to ruin a person's life comes from a man named Tony who lives in Southern

California. Tony lives with his wife in a recently remodeled Victorian-style home. This all-American couple loves their home and would never want to damage their credit rating or lose their equity through the foreclosure process. Tony and his wife only wanted to take advantage of some free government money.

When Tony and his wife heard about the Home Loan Modification Program, it sounded like a great deal. *Who wouldn't want lower house payments?* The only requirement for Tony to qualify would be to get a little behind on his mortgage payments. The couple even hired an attorney to help with the process. The attorney advised Tony to stop sending in mortgage payments and start sending the payments to his office. The attorney made it very clear that there was *no* guarantee that the mortgage company would agree to lower his principal balance, interest rates or even extend the term of his loan.

Unfortunately, Tony and his wife made a decision to stop sending in their mortgage payments and started sending the money to their attorney's office to pay for his services. As soon as Tony and his wife defaulted on their loan, the mortgage service provider started the foreclosure process. Because Tony lives in California, all the lender had to do was notify the homeowners and file a notice of foreclosure in the county records. Tony and his wife were totally unaware that their house was about to be sold at public auction, while they continued to place all their hope in their so-called attorney's efforts to negotiate a better deal on their behalf.

When Tony questioned his attorney about the wisdom of sending mortgage payments to his office instead of sending them to the lender, his attorney said, "If you stop sending me payments, I will stop the loan modification process."

When a member of our 2016 Christ-in-Congress Team spoke to Tony about his situation, Tony kept asking, "Should I call my attorney?" Ordinarily, the proper answer would be *yes!* Attorneys should be morally obligated to look out for their client's best interests. But when a self-proclaimed mortgage modification expert advises his clients to stop making payments in order to pay his own fees, someone needs to question his motives.

Fortunately for Tony's situation, he was able to see the wisdom in making all his payments in a timely manner. He began to realize that it was better to be a man of honor and integrity, a man who keeps his promises and commitments, a man who maintains God's favor and blessings, instead of trying to manipulate a lender to save some money at the taxpayers' expense.

After being informed about how the foreclosure process works, Tony stopped sending money to his attorney's office and started making his mortgage payments. Within a short period of time, Tony and his wife were able to bring their loan current and save their home from foreclosure. If it weren't for the intervention from the 2016 Christ-in-Congress Campaign, Tony and his wife would have been just two more victims of the Obama Administration's Home Loan Modification Program.

If you are wondering how Congress plans to help hundreds of thousands of homeowners who have been victimized and evicted from their homes while trusting in government assistance, the remedy involves spending more of our hard-earned tax dollars:

On November 1, 2011, federal regulators announced the start of a nationwide mortgage review program. The goal is to assist homeowners who have been treated unfairly by the nation's largest banks. To comply with this request, banks will be required to send out over four million letters to find people who have suffered harm due to the banks' mistakes and offer them compensation.

An article published by CNN describes the mortgage review process as follows: *When foreclosures flooded the system after the housing bust, many mortgage servicers became more cavalier in the way they handled foreclosures. Affidavits and other documents were signed by low-level employees who had little or no knowledge of what they were attesting to, attorneys hired to manage the foreclosure process were providing inadequate oversight and many bank employees were ignoring requirements to halt foreclosure procedures if loans were in the modification process.*[5]

All these problems started when the federal government created a program to help homeowners modify their mortgages. To implement this program, the Obama Administration paid large Wall Street banks like JPMorgan Chase, Wells Fargo and Citigroup billions of dollars. After these banks received the money, bank employees lost the vast amount of the applicants' modification paperwork; while at the same time, they continued to foreclose on more than four million homes.

After hundreds of thousands of complaints were filed, along with an extensive volume of lawsuits, the federal government is now asking banks to send out four million letters asking foreclosed homeowners if they have been unfairly treated—if they want to be compensated for their losses. As you can imagine, hundreds of thousands of angry homeowners will file a complaint with the federal government.

What do you think will happen next? Will the Obama Administration pay the banks more money to settle these claims? Will the federal government set up another save-the-day program to compensate millions of homeowners for their original loses? Or maybe the federal government should provide the homeowners a mortgage-free home, so they don't have to worry about making payments in the future.

Maybe a better question to ask is, Why should the American taxpayer support this?

CHAPTER THREE

WHAT CAN AMERICAN POLITICS DO FOR ME?

During an election campaign, there's usually a lot of talk in churches to *vote your conscience*. Because most churches operate under a 501(c)(3) public charity status, they are *not* allowed to get involved with politics. Although churches cannot endorse specific candidates, your local church can talk about issues facing the nation, encourage members to vote pro-life, or even encourage members to vote for the candidate that best represents their own ethics, values and morals.

Regardless of what church leaders say, most Americans will vote for their own personal benefit. If a single mother with three young children has been accumulating large medical bills, she will have a tendency to vote for the candidate who offers the best health care package, regardless of that candidates' view on abortion. College students that have been educated under a liberal worldview may be inclined to vote for the candidate who promises them legalized marijuana.

Because political candidates know that most Americans will vote for their pocketbooks, there has been a growing trend for politicians to offer the electorate everything they want to hear, along with a promise *not* to increase taxes. The question is, How can politicians offer free health care, free cash for clunkers, free home loan modifications, a $787 billion dollar economic stimulus package and a $447 billion jobs creation plan, and still not raise taxes?

To study the consequences of these actions, we need only to look at the riots in Greece. According to an article published by the BBC on May 6, 2010, *The Greek capital has been gripped by days of violent protests over government plans to slash public spending. Three people, including a pregnant woman, have been killed during riots in Athens.*

Why is Greece in such a mess? For years, Greece has been spending money it doesn't have. The government there took advantage of the economic good-times to borrow money and spend it on pay-raises for public workers and projects such as the 2004 Olympics. It began to run-up a bigger and bigger deficit (the gap between how much a country brings in from tax, and what it spends).

After the world economy went bad, Greece suffered. Banks started to view it as a country that might not be able to manage its debt. They worried Greece might eventually fail to pay its loans, and even go bankrupt. To cover the risk, banks started charging Greece more to borrow cash—making the problem even worse. Eventually the government there went looking for help. It is now borrowing 110 billion euros from other EU countries and the International Monetary Fund.[1]

Although the European Union and the International Monetary Fund offered Greece an attractive bailout package to prevent the country from defaulting on its loans; they also required Greece to make more than $30 billion of budget cuts over the next three years. The results of these actions have been described in an article published by the BBC on June 17, 2011, as follows:

This bailout came at a social cost. A harsh austerity program has resulted in public sector wage and benefit cuts, and a reduction in pensions, as well as an unemployment rate which has now climbed to 16%.

While spending has been cut, revenue-generating policies—including legislation to clamp down on tax evasion—have been enacted, but not really enforced. While restructuring and privatization programs have been met with great public hostility, the public debt is still growing. Public hostility against the austerity measures grows daily.[2]

At the time this book was written, Greece had been going through its debt crisis for several years. Many experts have been predicting that Greece will eventually withdraw from the Eurozone and default on its loans. Some have even predicted that Greece will try to acquire as much bailout money as possible from the European Union and International Monetary Fund before going into default.

By withdrawing from the Eurozone, Greece's government would be forced to reestablish its old currency (or release a new currency), thereby causing its citizens to suffer a greater financial loss. One day a Greek citizen could have $10,000 worth of buying power in his bank account, but after converting his assets into the new currency, he might only be able to purchase $2,000 worth of local goods. The unemployment rate in Greece could also reach 30 percent as more local businesses fail.

Other worst-case scenarios could include the seizure of government assets by foreign creditors and a civil war that could leave Greece in total chaos—all because politicians wanted to spend more money on programs than they collected in taxes.

A similar situation has also occurred in Spain. When Prime Minister José Luis Rodríguez Zapatero took office in 2004, the economy was booming. The Federal Reserve flooded the banks with easy money. Real estate prices had risen more than 200 percent between 1985 and 2007. Everybody was making money and getting rich off their credit cards and second mortgages.

During this time, Prime Minister Zapatero promoted a very liberal social agenda. According to an article published by *The Telegraph*, *Since coming to power in 2004, Jose Luis Rodriguez Zapatero has enacted radical social reforms that would once have been unthinkable in Spain—legalising gay marriages, relaxing divorce laws and reforming the abortion law.*

Some 20,000 gay couples have wed since the law, which also lets gay couples adopt children, making Spain the third member of the European Union after Belgium and the Netherlands to allow same-sex weddings.[3]

While the Socialist party in Spain was enjoying their newfound sexual freedoms and making money, they thought Prime Minister Zapatero was the best politician ever to take office. The party continued until the global financial crisis hit in 2008, creating more than a 21.5 percent unemployment rate in the third quarter of 2011.[4]

Now that housing prices in Spain have dropped 24 percent since their peak in 2007, and are expected to decline 35 and 40 percent over the next ten years, everybody in Spain is saying Prime Minister Zapatero was the worst politician ever!

Another example of what can happen to a country when big-government politicians take office by making unsustainable campaign promises comes from the Italian Prime Minister Silvio Berlusconi. According to an article published by the Associated Press on November 12, 2011, *Berlusconi stepped down amid jeers, cheers and heckles of "Buffoon" from thousands of people who packed downtown Rome to witness his government's downfall after a stunning week of market turmoil that upended his defiant hold on power and threatened to tear apart the eurozone.*

It was an ignoble end for the 75-year-old billionaire media mogul, who came to power for the first time in 1994 using a soccer chant "Let's Go Italy" as the name of his political party and selling Italians on a dream of prosperity with his own personal story of transformation from cruise-ship crooner to Italy's richest man.

While he became Italy's longest-serving post-war premier, Berlusconi's three stints as premier were tainted by corruption trials and accusations that he used his political power to help his business interests. His last term was marred by sex scandals, "bunga bunga" parties and criminal charges he paid a 17-year-old girl to have sex—accusations he denies.

Italy is under intense pressure to quickly put in place a new and effective government to replace him, one that *can push through even more painful reforms and austerity measures to deal with its staggering debts, which stand at $2.6 trillion, or a huge 120 percent of economic output. Italy has to roll over a little more than $410 billion of its debts next year alone.*

The yield on benchmark Italian 10-year bonds fell to 6.48 percent Friday, safely below the crisis level of 7 percent reached earlier this week. Greece, Ireland and Portugal all required international bailouts after their own borrowing rates passed 7 percent. The Italian economy would not be so easy to save. It totals $2 trillion, twice as much as the other three countries combined.

An Italian default could tear apart the coalition of 17 countries that use the euro as a common currency and deal a strong blow to the economies of Europe and the U.S., both trying to avoid recessions.[5]

After three terms in office, Prime Minister Berlusconi was finally driven from power by defecting party members, pressure from the financial markets and a possible payoff from the G-20 Summit. The question we need to consider is, Why would a country like Italy, with a 90 percent majority of Catholics, allow a seventy-five-year-old billionaire to remain in office amidst criminal allegations and sex scandals?

Some experts say that Berlusconi was able to stay in power because he controlled the media. Others say he paid large amounts of cash to buy confidence votes. Regardless of Berlusconi's wealth and power, why would a country composed of a 90 percent Catholic population not rise up and form a political opposition group? Because Italy is home to the Vatican, it would have been possible for the majority of Catholics to join together and put an end to Berlusconi's political career long before the "bunga bunga" parties started.

In the same way that Italy has a high percentage of Catholics, America has a high percentage of Christians. According to a recent report from the Pew Forum on Religion, America has a 76 percent Catholic/Christian population.[6] If the majority of Christians living in America would stop fighting among themselves, we could join together and put an end to the corruption in Washington. The breakdown for the religious population in America is as follows:

Religion	Percentage
Catholic	23.9
Baptist	17.2
Methodist	6.2
Protestant	4.9
Lutheran	4.6
Nondenominational	4.5
Pentecostal	4.4
Presbyterian	2.7
Evangelical	2.2
Church of Christ	1.5
Holiness	1.2
Episcopal	1
Congregational	.8
Orthodox	.6
Adventist	.5
Anglican	.3
Reformed	.3

Even though Christians have the power to join together and take control of Washington, some critics would say there needs to be *a separation between church and state.* This statement comes from the United States Constitution, which says, *Congress shall make no law respecting an establishment of religion or prohibiting the free exercise thereof.* This mandate means that the federal government cannot hinder (law-abiding) religious practices, nor can it promote or endorse any kind of religious doctrine. This does not mean that Christians should not get involved with politics.

Even though the vast majority of liberals and members of the LGBT movement (lesbian, gay, bi-sexual, transgender) would like to suppress Christian involvement with politics, God has given all Christians a mandate to transform the world. We are required by the Great Commission to make disciples of all nations, which would include the United States. We are called to be Ambassadors for Christ, to be light in a world of darkness and instruments of justice for the helpless and oppressed. We are called to promote good social order, restrain evil and promote God's ethics, values and morals in all aspects of life.

This directive began in Genesis 1:28 when God said, *"Be fruitful and multiply, and fill the earth and subdue it; and have dominion over the fish of the sea and over the birds of the air and over every living thing that moves upon the earth."*

After God placed the responsibility for the world's stewardship into our hands, he gave Moses a long list of moral, ethical and social laws as described in Exodus and Leviticus. These laws include a method for settling disputes, promoting good social order and other laws for governing ethical lending practices and sexual morality. When Moses was given these laws, he was also given the authority to settle disputes among the people.

Selecting Godly officials and judges to rule over a nation was such an effective way to promote good social order that the practice was later described in the book of Deuteronomy 16:18–20 as follows: *You shall appoint judges and officials throughout your tribes, in all your towns that the LORD your God is giving you, and they shall render just decisions for the people. You must not distort justice; you must not show partiality; and you must not accept bribes, for a bribe blinds the eyes of the wise and subverts the cause of those who are in the right. Justice, and only justice, you shall pursue, so that you may live and occupy the land that the LORD your God is giving you.*

When Christians fail to get involved in politics, ungodly men will creep into our government, and through the temptation of greed, power and deception, they will pass unethical laws, negotiate corrupt deals and pervert justice. A good example of the ever-growing presence of corruption that has consumed Washington comes from the scandal that occurred at Solyndra.

According to an article published by *The Chicago Tribune* on November 17, 2011, *The White House decision to back a California-based maker of advanced solar panels with a $535 million loan guarantee in 2009 looks seedier by the day. By all appearances, this deal and subsequent debacle had more to do with campaign cash and hoodwinking voters than it did with green energy.*

Solyndra Inc. burned through its loans in just two years, filed for bankruptcy and threw its employees on the street. If the story stopped there, it would be bad enough. But a trail of emails trickling out over recent months reveals much worse. The emails suggest that the Obama Administration put taxpayers on the hook for Solyndra without due diligence and then tried to hide the grim news about the company's impending failure right before the 2010 midterm election.

Just six months after Uncle Sam guaranteed the loan, the company was losing money so fast that its auditor voiced doubts about its ability to continue operations. Some White House staffers had questioned the wisdom of backing such a high-risk venture, but they were overruled.

This week, evidence surfaced at a congressional hearing that Energy Department officials pressed the company to delay a planned layoff until one day after the November 2010 midterm election. The obvious conclusion: the administration didn't want voters to know that the government's half-billion-dollar, signature green-energy investment was going belly up.[7]

In the case of Solyndra, the FBI was called in to investigate, but because President Obama has only granted Robert Mueller a two-year extension to oversee the FBI, it's unlikely that any wrongdoing will ever be disclosed to the public. Energy Secretary Steven Chu has already testified before Congress and has not admitted any kind of wrongdoing. According to an article published by ABC News, *Chu claimed he was looking out for the taxpayer all along when reviewing the Solyndra finances.*

"As the Secretary of Energy, the final decisions on Solyndra were mine, and I made them with the best

interest of the taxpayer in mind," Chu said in testimony before the House Energy and Commerce Committee. *"And I want to be clear: over the course of Solyndra's loan guarantee, I did not make any decision based on political considerations."*[8]

If you were part of the 2016 Christ-in-Congress Presidential Team, how would you deal with these types of scandals? Would you allow the federal government to take $528 million dollars ($528,000,000) of taxpayer money and loan it to a private company? Would you consider this to be in the "best interest" of the taxpayer? Two years after receiving the money, the executives at Solyndra spent every penny on themselves and then declared bankruptcy.

The only ethical solution would be to send in an army of accountants and lawyers to figure out what really happened. Once all the facts have been uncovered, arrest warrants could be issued, assets could be seized and the stolen money could be returned to its rightful owners. Those who were found guilty of committing crimes by a court of law would be brought to justice, and the victims would receive a fair amount of compensation for their damages.

If you are wondering why the federal government doesn't want to pursue the taxpayer's lost money, it may have something to do with one of President Obama's campaign supporters. According to an article published by *The Chicago Tribune*, *A big Obama donor—Oklahoma billionaire George Kaiser—may have played a pivotal role in securing the government financing. He discussed Solyndra with the White House as the company tried to get even more taxpayer backing and stave off collapse. Unable to secure a second government loan, Kaiser and fellow investors made a private loan—but they moved ahead of taxpayers in line for repayment when Solyndra defaulted.*[9]

If you were part of the 2016 Christ-in-Congress Presidential Team, would you be willing to uphold justice by enforcing our existing laws? Would you be willing to pass new anti-corruption laws for all publicly elected officials? Would you support legislation that prevented corporations from influencing a federal election and limit the amount of individual expenditures?

According to a list of 2008 campaign contributors, several Wall Street banks have been identified as President Obama's top supporters.[10] *It's important to note that these organizations themselves did not donate; rather, the money came from the organizations' PACs, their individual members or employees or owners, and those individuals' immediate families.* The list reads as follows:

Wall Street Banks	Campaign Donations
Goldman Sachs	$1,013,091.00
JPMorgan Chase	$808,799.00
Citigroup Inc	$736,771.00
UBS AG	$532,674.00
Morgan Stanley	$512,232.00

In addition to receiving large campaign donations from Wall Street banks, large oil companies also spent a lot of money on Congress. According to an article published by Politico on May 5, 2010, *While the BP oil geyser pumps millions of gallons of petroleum into the Gulf of Mexico, President Barack Obama and members of*

Congress may have to answer for the millions in campaign contributions they've taken from the oil and gas giant over the years.

BP and its employees have given more than $3.5 million to federal candidates over the past 20 years, with the largest chunk of their money going to Obama, according to the Center for Responsive Politics. Donations come from a mix of employees and the company's political action committees—$2.89 million flowed to campaigns from BP-related PACs and about $638,000 came from individuals. On top of that, the oil giant has spent millions each year on lobbying—including $15.9 million last year alone—as it has tried to influence energy policy.[11]

It would appear the problem with our current government is the vast amount of greed and corruption that flows between Washington and Wall Street—that somehow an elite group of billionaires has taken control of our nation. As these powerful billionaires continue to pillage our nation, the average hard-working American struggles under high unemployment rates, lower paying jobs, increased debt and never-ending government scandals, all while paying 30 to 36 percent in taxes.

If in the event you do not like the direction our nation is heading, there's hope for America. If the majority of Christians living in America joined forces in the 2016 Christ-in-Congress Campaign, we could push back enemy lines for a very long time.

PART TWO
THE SOLUTION

CHAPTER FOUR

REMOVE CORRUPT POLITICIANS FROM OFFICE

At the time this book was written, several Republican candidates were running against President Obama for the 2012 elections. Mitt Romney appeared to be in the lead, or the candidate most favored by the national media. The other candidates seemed to be under severe attack. Newt Gingrich was being questioned on why he received more than $1.6 million in consulting fees from Freddie Mac and Fannie Mae, the two federal mortgage giants who were responsible for bringing down the housing market in 2008.

According to an article published by *Bloomberg News* on November 16, 2011, *Newt Gingrich made between $1.6 million and $1.8 million in consulting fees from two contracts with mortgage company Freddie Mac, according to two people familiar with the arrangement. The total amount is significantly larger than the $300,000 payment from Freddie Mac that Gingrich was asked about during a Republican presidential debate on Nov. 9 sponsored by CNBC, and more than was disclosed in the middle of congressional investigations into the housing industry collapse.*[1]

The Freddie Mac officials also told Bloomberg that Gingrich was asked to build bridges with Capitol Hill Republicans and help sell the mortgage company's public-private structure to conservatives.

While campaigning in Iowa this week, the former House Speaker disputed these claims by saying, *"I do no lobbying of any kind, and I offered strategic advice and that's all I do," Gingrich said. "I don't go to the Hill. I don't lobby in any way. I haven't for the years I've left the speakership, period."* [2]

The other candidates who were under heavy attack by the media were Rick Perry and Herman Cain. Rick Perry was being assaulted because of what the press called "poor debate performance." Apparently he couldn't remember a few facts, or maybe he paused a moment too long when thinking about one of the media's trick questions, and he was portrayed as someone who stutters and forgets where he left his car keys.

Herman Cain was also under heavy attack from the media for alleged sexual harassment complaints and cash settlements paid to women while he was CEO of the National Restaurant Association. Every time the media mentioned Herman Cain's name, they continued to bring up the sexual allegations. The other candidates were Michele Bachmann, Ron Paul, Rick Santorum, Jon Huntsman and Gary Johnson.

At this point in time, it would appear that Mitt Romney will run as the Republican candidate against President Obama. As soon as Mitt is nominated for the Republican Party, it's safe to assume the media will turn their focus and efforts against him so that President

Obama can be reelected for another term in office. During his second term, 76 percent of Christians living in America will have numerous reasons to complain about the damage the Obama Administration is causing our nation by advancing the homosexual movement, funding Planned Parenthood offices inside public schools, and taking more congressional action to stimulate the economy.

It seems like every four years, the majority of Christians living in America find themselves perplexed at the choices set before them as presidential candidates. Yet time and time again we continue to elect our presidents from the same pool of career politicians. If in the event you would like to see a group of Godly men take control of Washington, there's hope for America in the 2016 Christ-in-Congress Campaign. First, let's discuss what it means to be a Godly man from a biblical perspective:

1. The first requirement is to be a born-again, Spirit-filled disciple of the Lord, Jesus Christ. There are plenty of political candidates who have some sort of religious affiliation, but religious affiliation or church attendance doesn't necessarily make a man Godly. A Godly man will need to confess Jesus as his Lord and Savior. This means a man has to acknowledge he is a sinner in need of a savior. Because the penalty for sin is death, every man has a choice to make—he can pay the death penalty himself, or he can ask Jesus to pay the death penalty on his behalf. Once a man chooses Jesus as Savior, he will be granted access to God's thrown room through prayer, so that he can be filled with the Holy Spirit.

2. The second requirement is to live a life in partnership with God's Spirit. Because God doesn't fill sinful men with his Spirit, the process of sanctification begins when a man removes all forms of seductive temptations from his life. A Godly man will need to invite the power of the Holy Spirit into his heart to eliminate his desire for sin. He will need to search deep within his heart, uncover all the devil's lies, and replace those lies with God's truth. He will need to replace his own selfish agenda with a desire to know, love and serve God.

3. After a Godly man spends many years working in partnership with the Holy Spirit—removing seductive temptations from his life—he can then start advancing God's kingdom here on earth. You can find Godly men in all walks of life serving the Lord in many different industries. Some serve as doctors, lawyers and experts in law, others serve as priests, pastors and missionaries. The Bible says we can identify a Godly man by his fruit. When a Godly man spends a lifetime working together with God's Spirit, we should be able to look into his life and see an abundant harvest.

4. Another requirement for a Godly man is to have a servant's heart. A good servant has a desire to serve his Lord as Master, unlike many of today's political leaders who are only concerned with their own agenda. A Godly man realizes that he has to put his fleshly desires to death in order to serve Christ. According to Jesus, *"Unless a grain of wheat falls into the earth and dies, it remains just a single grain; but if it dies, it bears much fruit."*[3] The process of dying to self requires an ongoing effort and a very serious prayer life. Once a man starts working together with God's Spirit to overcome selfishness, he can then focus his efforts on accomplishing God's will.

5. Being able to operate in God's truth is another important requirement for political leaders. Many of today's politicians think truth is situational, meaning that one form of truth applies to one situation, while a different version of truth may be more appropriate for another situation. From a worldly perspective, this may seem like a good answer—that truth is something a person creates for himself. Pontius Pilate had the same problem when Jesus was brought before him. When Jesus said, *"Everyone who belongs to the truth listens to my voice,"*[4] Pilate responded by saying, *"What is truth?"*[5]

Before Pilate could discern God's truth, he first had to be filled with God's Spirit. Only a Godly man filled with God's Spirit can access God's truth, because it flows into a man's heart directly from God. Those born of God's Spirit know the truth, and those who do not know God, cannot discern the truth. Being able to operate in the truth is such an important requirement for Godly leaders that as soon as a man tells one little lie, it will grieve God's Spirit to the point where God's presence may depart from his life.

When this happens, a Godly man will immediately confess his sin and make amends for his actions. When a man fails to confess his sins, he opens the door to the demonic, and by doing so, the demonic spirits will help him cover the first lie with more lies. A good example of this comes from the time when President Bill Clinton testified before Congress by saying, *I did not have sex with that woman.* From a worldly perspective, this form of truth may depend on how Congress defines the word *sex,* but from God's perspective, sexual infidelity between a married man and a single woman is a very serious sin.

Now that we have defined a few characteristics for being a Godly man, let's look at some biblical examples of Godly leaders from Sacred Scripture. When King Nebuchadnezzar of Babylon came to Jerusalem to besiege it, the Lord let Judah fall under his power. A command was issued for the palace master *to bring some of the Israelites of the royal family and of the nobility, young men without physical defect and handsome, versed in every branch of wisdom, endowed with knowledge and insight, and competent to serve in the king's palace; they were to be taught the literature and language of the Chaldeans.*

The king assigned them a daily portion of the royal rations of food and wine. They were to be educated for three years, so that at the end of that time they could be stationed in the king's court. Among them were Daniel, Hananiah, Mishael, and Azariah, from the tribe of Judah.[6]

Daniel resolved that he would not defile himself with the royal rations of food and wine; so he asked the palace master to allow him not to defile himself. Now God allowed Daniel to receive favor and compassion from the palace master. The palace master said to Daniel, "I am afraid of my lord the king; he has appointed your food and your drink. If he should see you in poorer condition than the other young men of your own age, you would endanger my head with the king."[7]

"Please test your servants for ten days. Let us be given vegetables to eat and water to drink. You can then compare our appearance with the appearance of the young men who eat the royal rations, and deal with your servants according to what you observe."

So he agreed to this proposal and tested them for

ten days. At the end of ten days it was observed that they appeared better and fatter than all the young men who had been eating the royal rations. So the guard continued to withdraw their royal rations and the wine they were to drink, and gave them vegetables. To these four young men God gave knowledge and skill in every aspect of literature and wisdom; Daniel also had insight into all visions and dreams.[8]

The first characteristic that we see in the lives of these Godly men was a desire to fast. Daniel and his companions would rather eat vegetables and water than enjoy a banquet of fine wines and rich foods from the king's table. While all the other young men were enjoying the finer things in life, Daniel and his companions were praying and fasting, seeking God's approval; and because they did so, God rewarded them with the wisdom, knowledge and understanding they needed to advance in excellence.

At the end of the three-year training period, Daniel and his companions needed to be tested before they could serve in the king's court. *The palace master brought them into the presence of Nebuchadnezzar, and the king spoke with them. And among them all, no one was found to compare with Daniel, Hananiah, Mishael, and Azariah; therefore they were stationed in the king's court. In every matter of wisdom and understanding concerning which the king inquired of them, he found them ten times better than all the magicians and enchanters in his whole kingdom.[9]*

After Daniel and his companions rose to a position of political power within the government, King Nebuchadnezzar had a dream that he wanted his wise men to interpret. If the king disclosed the dream to his court attendances in advance, they may have told him anything that he wanted to hear. Knowing that his court attendants viewed truth as situational, something to be created for any occasion, the king wanted them to first disclose the dream, so that he knew the interpretation would be correct.

Upon hearing this, *the Chaldeans answered the king, "There is no one on earth who can reveal what the king demands! In fact no king, however great and powerful, has ever asked such a thing of any magician or enchanter or Chaldean. The thing that the king is asking is too difficult, and no one can reveal it to the king except the gods, whose dwelling is not with mortals."*

Because of this the king flew into a violent rage and commanded that all the wise men of Babylon be destroyed. The decree was issued, and the wise men were about to be executed; and they looked for Daniel and his companions, to execute them.

Then Daniel responded with prudence and discretion to Arioch, the king's chief executioner, who had gone out to execute the wise men of Babylon; he asked Arioch, the royal official, "Why is the decree of the king so urgent?" Arioch then explained the matter to Daniel. So Daniel went in and requested that the king give him time and he would tell the king the interpretation.

Then Daniel went to his home and informed his companions, Hananiah, Mishael, and Azariah, and told them to seek mercy from the God of heaven concerning this mystery, so that Daniel and his companions with the rest of the wise men of Babylon might not perish. Then the mystery was revealed to Daniel in a vision of the night, and Daniel blessed the God of heaven.[10]

In this situation, we can see Daniel and his companions seeking the necessary wisdom and insight into a very serious political problem. No ordinary man could produce such knowledge. Even the most educated and crafty politician could not disclose the king's dream. The answer, like the solutions to all our world's problems, needed to come from God. After Daniel and his companions prayed and fasted, God was more than happy to give them all the wisdom they needed.

Another Godly characteristic that we see demonstrated in the life of Daniel was his ability to take a stand for righteousness in the face of adversity. When King Darius issued a law prohibiting prayer for thirty days, Daniel and his companions continued to persevere in honor and integrity to the point of risking their own lives. Daniel could have stopped praying to God, but instead he continued maintaining his relationship with the King of all kings. Because Daniel continued to walk in integrity, God rewarded him with all the wisdom, power and protection that he needed to govern a nation.

A modern-day example of our political leaders' need to stand up for righteousness in the face of adversity comes from the sub-prime mortgage crisis. Between 2002 and 2006 the real estate market was booming. People were flipping condos within a few weeks after buying them. Investors could obtain a non-qualifying loan with no income verification or credit report, buy a condo and sell it a month later for a $10,000 profit.

Federal agencies like the U.S. Department of

Housing and Urban Development, Freddie Mac, Fannie Mae and Ginnie Mae would then bundle these loans together in huge pools and sell them to foreign investors. The foreign investors didn't have any problems buying these mortgages because they were explicitly backed by the full faith of the U.S. Government. In the event of a default, the federal government would guarantee the buyer's *principal and interest payments on the outstanding securities in a timely manner.*[11]

Before the real estate boom turned into a bubble, someone should have taken a stand. Someone in our government should have been able to look around, knowing that for every boom there would be a bust; and for every over-inflated bubble, there would be a correction. The question is, Where were all our Godly leaders, men of integrity like Daniel and his companions who would have taken a stand for righteousness in the face of adversity?

Apparently, our current political leaders didn't see anything wrong with the real estate boom—everybody was making money and everything seemed fine. Newt Gingrich was receiving $1.6 million ($1,600,000) in what he calls "consultation fees" from Freddie Mac and Fannie Mae, yet he doesn't want to acknowledge any kind of wrongdoing. He only wants people to vote for him in 2012 so he can be our next president.

If you are wondering what results the 2016 Christ-in-Congress Presidential Team could produce for our nation, the possibilities are endless. The first goal would be to set up a public referendum platform. The new referendum platform could be used in a number of ways. For example, if Congress was working on a health care reform bill, the American people could login to the site to express their opinion on specific questions.

One question our Presidential Team could ask the American people is, Do you want a health care law that's legally binding on all Americans? *This would mean a law that requires all Americans to obtain a certain level of coverage, or else face financial penalties imposed by the Internal Revenue Service.* If the majority of Americans said *no*, then it would serve as a guide to direct Congress on which direction to proceed.

Another use for the referendum platform would be a formal vote conducted by all the states. According to an article published on October 8, 2007, *Referendums are an important tool for allowing the will of the people to be expressed, say two U.S. public policy analysts.*

Dennis Polhill, in a 2006 article for the Initiative and Referendum Institute at the University of Southern California, advocated putting referendums on a U.S. national ballot. Polhill, a member of the institute's board of directors, said national referendums would offer a way to address national issues that "partisan politics" block.

Several attempts have been made to establish a national referendum system in the United States to no avail, said Polhill. But he added that as "citizens enlarge their participation in their government, it appears inevitable" that the United States "will find a way to exercise this fundamental right in the near future."[12]

One of the first referendums that our 2016 Christ-in-Congress Presidential Team could put before the electorate (rather than going through their representatives) would be new anti-corruption legislation for all public officials. These new laws would make it illegal for all publicly elected officials to accept any form of bribes, fees or payments other than the compensation they receive through their government salaries. For example, the $1.6 million consulting fees Newt Gingrich received from Freddie Mac and Fannie Mae for "building bridges with Capitol Hill Republicans" would be considered illegal.

The new anti-corruption laws would also make insider trading illegal for all members of Congress and their staff. A good example of how members of Congress are able to use privileged information to make bets in the stock markets comes from an article published on November 16, 2011, that says, *Whether you are Republican or Democrat, an occupier or a tea partyist, the report last Sunday by CBS' "60 Minutes" on insider trading by members of Congress should have steam whistling from your ears.*

The most egregious example cited by CBS was U.S. Rep. Spencer Bachus of Alabama, who three years ago was the ranking Republican on the House banking committee, and is now its chairman. In September 2008, Bachus and other congressional leaders were privately briefed by Treasury Secretary Hank Paulson and Federal Reserve Chairman Ben Bernanke on the economy's imminent meltdown.

The next day, Bachus was buying option funds that would increase in value if the economy tanked. It did. While your 401(k) and all thoughts of retirement melted into a never-ending job at Wal-Mart, the House chairman made a tidy profit on his country's misfortunes.[13]

The new anti-corruption laws would also make it illegal for publicly elected officials (and their close family members) to buy assets below fair market value. For example, if a large oil company wanted to sell $20 million worth of oil wells to a member of Congress for $10,000 (in an attempt to build bridges with Republicans), the transaction would be considered illegal.

These new anti-corruption laws would also require that our publicly elected officials' financial records be subject to annual audits. For example, if a man entered public office with a net worth of $1 million, and received an annual government salary of $100,000, at the end of the year, his net assets should not exceed $1.1 million.

If during the audit process the politician's net worth increased to more than $15 million, he would have to prove how he bought and sold assets at fair-market value to account for the difference. If the politician tried to hide money in offshore bank accounts, he could face time in prison in addition to having his assets confiscated. If a large oil company tried to sell assets to a politician's family member below fair-market value, they too, could be liable to prosecution.

Critics may argue that these new anti-corruption laws would hinder a politician's freedom—that our politicians have been hired to work a full-time job representing the American people—yet they should be able to engage in $1.6 million consulting deals, write books to earn royalties and day-trade the stock markets using insider information.

In response to these objections, what do you think would happen if an employee at a private company spent the majority of his time acting in this manner? If an employee at a private firm was paid $174,000 per year and given a multimillion-dollar expense account, would he not be expected to remain focused on his full-time responsibilities? If he spent his time accepting bribes, negotiating corrupt deals and producing dysfunctional results for his employer, would he not be fired immediately?

The following chart shows the salaries for the members of Congress. In addition to these salaries, they also receive health insurance, life insurance and retirement provisions. Members of Congress also receive millions of dollars for office and clerical staff assistance. U.S. representatives are allowed to spend $944,671 per year and hire up to eighteen staff members, each with a pay cap set at $168,411 per year. They are also allowed to spend $256,574 per year for office and travel expenses.[14]

A senator's office expense ranges between $128,585 to $465,922 per year, depending on how far their home state is located from Washington, D.C. A senator's employee allowance varies between $2,512,574 for states with a population under five million, and $3,993,206 for states with a population over twenty-eight million.[15] The current pay schedule for Congress is as follows:

Effective Dates	Salaries for Congress
January 1, 2001	$145,100.00
January 1, 2002	$150,000.00
January 1, 2003	$154,700.00
January 1, 2004	$158,100.00
January 1, 2005	$162,100.00
January 1, 2006	$165,200.00
January 1, 2007	$165,200.00
January 1, 2008	$169,300.00
January 1, 2009	$174,000.00
January 1, 2010	$174,000.00
January 1, 2011	$174,000.00
January 1, 2012	$174,000.00

CHAPTER FIVE

A MIGHTY ARMY TO ADVANCE GOD'S KINGDOM

To begin the 2016 Christ-in-Congress Campaign, we would first need to send a message throughout America. We will need to conduct a search for a few Godly men who would be willing to earn $174,000 per year serving the Lord, fighting evil and promoting justice. The easiest way to broadcast this message would be through the secular media, but because the secular media would be very hostile to a Christian movement, we would need to find another way. King Saul faced a similar problem when an evil army invaded Israel.

Before Saul assumed his role as king, he was confronted by the invasion of the Ammonite army who besieged one of Israel's towns named Jabesh-gilead. The men from that region tried to make a deal with their oppressors by saying, *"Make a treaty with us, and we will serve you."*

But Nahash the Ammonite said to them, *"On this condition I will make a treaty with you, namely that I gouge out everyone's right eye, and thus put disgrace upon all Israel."*

The elders of Jabesh said to him, *"Give us seven days'*

respite that we may send messengers through all the territory of Israel. Then, if there is no one to save us, we will give ourselves up to you." When the messengers came to Gibeah of Saul, they reported the matter in the hearing of the people; and all the people wept aloud.

Now Saul was coming from the field behind the oxen; and Saul said, "What is the matter with the people, that they are weeping?" So they told him the message from the inhabitants of Jabesh. And the spirit of God came upon Saul in power when he heard these words, and his anger was greatly kindled.

He took a yoke of oxen, and cut them in pieces and sent them throughout all the territory of Israel by messengers, saying, "Whoever does not come out after Saul and Samuel, so shall it be done to his oxen!" Then the dread of the Lord fell upon the people, and they came out as one.[1]

Three hundred thousand men from Israel reported for battle along with seventy thousand men from Judah. A vast army of mighty warriors came together within a few days to fight an evil force that had invaded their territory. Saul told the citizens from the besieged town to pretend as if they would surrender. The leaders from that region said to their oppressors, *"Tomorrow we will give ourselves up to you, and you may do to us whatever seems good to you."[2]*

Upon hearing this, the Ammonite army rejoiced at the possibility of gouging out everybody's right eye. Meanwhile, Saul and his army of warriors divided their troops into three sections. *At the morning watch they came into the camp and cut down the Ammonites until the heat of the day; and those who survived were scattered, so that no two of them were left together.[3]*

In the same way that all the mighty warriors of Israel were able to come together to purge an evil force from their land, so too, will all the Godly men and women in America need to come together to drive evil out of our government.

A good example of the power that Christians possess to accomplish God's agenda comes from the Promise Keepers Million Man March: *On October 4, 1997, Promise Keepers hosted "Stand in the Gap: A Sacred Assembly of Men" on the National Mall in Washington, D.C. The day opened as Jewish shofars sounded to commence the program. An estimated one million men participated in "Stand in the Gap," a day of personal repentance and prayer. The event gathered men from every race, nationality, and most Christian denominations as well as from many countries around the world.*[4]

Instead of a million men gathering in Washington, D.C. for a day of prayer, we will need a million-man army of mighty warriors who are to willing to fight the evil, greed and corruption that has crept into our government. We will need an army of Godly leaders, accountants and lawyers to pursue all the taxpayers' dollars that have been improperly consumed by Solyndra, MF Global and other Wall Street firms.

We will need an army of public defenders and attorneys to pursue and bring to justice all the corrupt deals that have transpired behind closed doors in Washington. We will need thousands of Godly administrators to oversee and monitor all our existing government programs. We will need Godly judges to replace those who have been accepting bribes and buying multimillion-dollar houses on a public servant's salary.

From the time this book was written, we have five years to prepare for the war between good and evil in American politics. During the next couple years, our goal would be to conduct thousands of town hall meetings. We will need to mobilize a mighty army of evangelists to implement a nationwide door-to-door program.

The purpose for the door-to-door evangelization program is for Christians to meet all the neighbors who live on the same block, apartment building or condo unit. In many suburban neighborhoods, most Christians don't even know their neighbors' names. They may wave to one another on occasion, or say hello, but other than that, most Americans have become very isolated. Our society's form of social interaction has been reduced to text messages, e-mails and virtual dating sites.

From God's perspective, it's very important for Christians to know their neighbors. To begin, all you need to do is knock on a few doors. After some neighborly introductions have been made, you can speak to your neighbors about the condition of our world and the growing concern you have for American politics. If President Obama is reelected for another four years, you will have plenty to talk about, because every week there will be another scandal dominating the evening news.

After taking a moment to talk to your neighbors about the growing political scandals our nation is facing, you can ask your neighbors' advice in regards to solving these problems. After listening to everything your neighbor has to say, you could then share your vision for the 2016 Christ-in-Congress Campaign. If your neighbor is interested in being part of the movement, it would give you an opportunity to share your faith. If your neighbor doesn't know Jesus as Savior, you would have the opportunity to introduce your neighbor to Jesus through prayer. Maybe you could even invite your neighbor to church on Sunday morning.

The underlying purpose for the door-to-door campaign is evangelization. God is more concerned with the salvation of souls than he is with American politics. God wants every household in America to hear the Gospel Message. God wants to see Christians reach out to their neighbors in love, listen and pray for the struggles and difficulties they maybe facing. Once Christians start doing the work God has called them to do, God will be more than happy to raise up an army of warriors to clean the filth out of Washington.

You can start the door-to-door evangelization program immediately, and it won't cost you any money. You don't even need your church's approval. All you need to do is pray and seek God's guidance. Ask God a simple question: *Do you want me to meet all my neighbors?* If God says *yes,* then you will have God's blessing and favor when you step out in faith to accomplish his will. Once you meet a few people, you can start praying for your neighbors' needs to see how God blesses them.

To help accomplish the goal of reaching every household in America, the 2016 Christ-in-Congress Campaign will also run radio and television advertisements. Every year Americans donate millions of dollars to political campaigns, and most of that money is spent on slanderous commercials. Instead of supporting an ungodly slander campaign, all of our Christ-in-Congress advertisements will contain the Gospel Message.

Our bumper stickers have the cross of Christ firmly affixed on top of the capital building. The same concept is being used in radio and television commercials. In every form of public advertisement, we have a desire to proclaim the Gospel Message so that unbelievers in America will once again be reminded of their need to repent and accept Jesus as Savior.

The majority of Christian radio and television stations would be willing to promote the 2016 Christ-in-Congress Campaign for very little cost, but when it comes time to deal with the secular media, our candidates will need to be very careful. A good example of the media's hostility toward Christians comes from Sarah Palin's vice presidential nomination with John McCain in 2008.

In a book entitled, *Sarah from Alaska,* two embedded reporters who traveled with the campaign described the press coverage as follows: *Despite the enormous national interest in all things Palin, her traveling press corps was notably smaller than the presidential candidates', with no more than twenty members of the media on most flights and a core group of one embedded reporter/ producer from each of the five television networks. No wire service or newspaper reporters traveled regularly, and NBC was the only network that devoted a correspondent and full crew to Palin coverage around the clock.*[5]

In a chapter entitled "The Iron Curtain," the embedded reporters described how they had to sit in the back of the plane while Sarah and her campaign managers sat in the front rows: *The conspicuous gray curtains were a psychological barrier as well as a physical one. They divided the plane into two zones that sometimes seemed, in the heat of the mentally exhausting campaign, as estranged as West and East Berlin once were. None of the reporters could say for sure what went on in the front of the plane, but they had a pretty good idea that life was a little better up there, especially during meals.[6]*

The curtains were not a bona fide reason why the relationship between the campaign and the media became particularly antagonistic in the first half of Palin's candidacy, but they did not exactly set a positive tone. They were always tightly drawn, except during takeoffs and landings when FAA regulations required that they be opened. It was as if the campaign's handlers were concerned that a deranged New York Times *reporter might leap from his seat, sprint down the aisle to the front of the plane, and demand of Palin whether she knew both ways to pronounce "Qatar."[7]*

During the long hours that the embedded reporters sat in the back of the plane, they would spend time trying to craft clever questions in an attempt to stump the candidates. For example, one of the CBS News reporters suggested a foreign policy question about how the United States should respond in the event of a Chinese attack on Taiwan by saying, *"With doubts continuing to swirl about Palin's knowledge of international affairs, it seemed like a good opportunity to test how deeply she had thought about a critical, yet less talked-about, region of the world."[8]*

Another example of the secular media's ability to craft trick questions comes from a debate where a moderator asked Herman Cain, "Do you agree with the way President Obama handled the war in Libya?" If Herman Cain answered *yes*, the reporters would attack him by saying that President Obama went to war without receiving approval from Congress. If Herman Cain answered *no*, the reporters would attack him by saying that the Libyan people were being slaughtered by an evil dictator—someone needed to assume a leadership role to protect them!

The proper answer would be to break down the reporter's trick questions into a list of all of President Obama's actions concerning Libya and then to discuss each of those actions separately. Unfortunately, this would not be possible when reporters ask hypothetical questions, because there could be a thousand real-life scenarios that would affect the proper answer. For example, how should the United States respond to an attack on Taiwan by China?

The proper answer would be to discuss the situation with senior military officials, discuss the situation with international leaders, discuss the situation with Congress, discuss the situation with the American people, pray about all the details, discern God's will for the situation and take the appropriate actions.

Another example of the secular media's hostility toward Christians comes from Sarah Palin's book, *Going Rogue*, where she describes her interview with CBS's television news anchor Katie Couric. Sarah describes the interview by saying, *On the bus, the topic turned to social issues. Katie asked me if I thought it was possible to "pray away gay"—to convert homosexuals to heterosexuality through prayer. Hmmm, I thought. Odd question. I don't think she really wanted to hear my answer because she interrupted me five times as I tried to give it. The badgering had begun. This is really annoying me, I thought. Then she* asked me about abortion and the morning-after pill twelve times. Twelve different times.

I answered as graciously and as patiently as I could. Each time, I reiterated my pro-life, pro-woman, pro-adoption position. But no matter how many ways I tried to say it, Katie responded by asking her question again in a slightly different way. The line of questioning began, of course, with an extreme, horrific example: "If a fifteen-year-old is raped by her father, you believe it should be illegal for her to get an abortion. Why?"

I answered there were good people on both sides of the abortion debate, but that I was unapologetically pro-life, and that I would counsel someone to choose life. I also said that we should build a culture of life in which we help women in difficult situations, encourage adoption, and support foster and adoptive families.

Katie jumped in, "But, ideally, you think it should be illegal..."

I answered again: I would personally counsel such a girl to choose life, despite these horrific circumstances, but I absolutely didn't think anyone should end up in jail for having an abortion. Katie included that but didn't include another important part of my answer: that we should support women in these difficult circumstances and give them the resources necessary to give their children life.[9]

But that wasn't enough. Katie asked it again. And again. And again. I had been out of journalism for a long time, and it was pretty obvious the rules had changed. I felt sick about the depths to which some in the press had apparently sunk, not because it was unfair to me and John, but because it was unfair to the American electorate.[10]

I couldn't have known it then, but what transpired during the series of interviews and what CBS actually aired were two different breeds of cat.

Camera crews shot hours of footage across the U.S.; Katie and her producers decided on which fraction America would see—and let's just say the emphasis was on my worst moments. Editing footage is nothing new, of course; I created video packages when I worked as a sports reporter. But responsible editing means you keep substance and context, and trim out fat. When I saw the final cut, it was clear that CBS had sought out the bad moments, and systematically sliced out material that would accurately convey my message. The sin of omission was glaring.[11]

One way to prevent this type of media coverage would be to record all the secular media's interviews with our own film crew. That way if reporters like Katie Couric keep asking members of our Presidential Team trick questions over and over again, we would have the interview on film. If CBS released a chopped-up version showing the candidates' aggravation at their badgering and biased questions, we could show the real story of what actually transpired.

This approach would also make the 2016 Christ-in-Congress Campaign more interesting. When reporters like Katie Couric tried to attack our candidates with badgering questions about abortion, members of our own film crew could ask Katie Couric a few questions like: *Do you know what the Bible says about fornication? And how many abortions have you had in the past?* That way, the interviews would be more interactive, real and dynamic.

Another option for dealing with the secular media would be to ask for a list of questions in advance. If CBS reporters were *really* interested in our candidate's views on abortion, homosexuality or pornography, we could record an interview at a Christian television studio and then release the footage to the public. Another option would be to make the secular media sign a contract with provisions for releasing only pre-approved footage.

Maybe the best option for dealing with the secular media would be to avoid them all together. If the majority of Christians living in America conducted a successful door-to-door campaign, we would not need any secular television interviews.

Once our 2016 Christ-in-Congress Presidential Team takes control of the White House, we will start working on the issues facing America. The first priority would be to create the public referendum platform. The next agenda would be to pass strict anti-corruption laws and start removing corrupt politicians from office. We will also need to create a thriving economy without government stimulus and establish affordable health care without taxpayer-funded abortions.

Other issues would include supporting a strong military to keep our country safe, yet at the same time, establishing a foreign policy that transforms the world, outlawing pornographic images from the public domain and upholding our nation's ethics, values and morals.

CHAPTER SIX

CREATING A THRIVING ECONOMY WITHOUT GOVERNMENT STIMULUS

Four years after the global financial crisis, all the American people have been hearing about is the bad economy. Every night on the evening news, the unemployment rate is over 9 percent, millions of Americans can't find jobs, the housing market is in freefall, hundreds of thousands of homeowners are in foreclosure, and there's even talk of a double-dip recession.

Our current government's response has been to either borrow more money or devalue our currency to stimulate the economy. Because Federal Reserve Chairman Ben Bernanke has the ability to create money out of thin air, he wants to turn on the printing presses, while President Obama's plan involves raising the federal deficit. Neither of these strategies seems to be helping, nor do they address the underlying issues facing the nation.

A good example of President Obama's efforts to stimulate the economy comes from his American Jobs Act. According to an article published by *The Washington Post* on September 8, 2011, *President Obama urged Congress Thursday night to pass a $447 billion plan that* *he said will get the economy moving and create jobs.*[1]

After making his request to Congress, President Obama started touring the country making speeches trying to rally public support. He wants everybody to apply pressure to members of Congress to "Pass this bill right away!" According to an article by the Associated Press, *Obama promoted his package anew in his Saturday radio and internet address, saying the mix of tax cuts and direct spending would put tens of thousands of teachers back to work and modernize at least 35,000 schools.*[2] His plan also includes the *building of bridges, roads and highways* that will put tens of thousands of construction workers back on the job!

All this may sound very good to the average citizen, but if you have a construction background, you know that bridge and highway construction is very specialized work. The majority of unemployed construction workers come from the residential housing market, which includes plumbers, electricians, roofers, framers, painters and carpet installers. There are only a few contractors in every state who can build bridges or highways, and most of these contractors don't need any more work.

The majority of state, federal and local government construction projects are open to the public bid process. Anyone with the required experience, equipment, manpower, financing and insurance can bid on a federal bridge or highway project. Because the average carpet installer and cabinet maker does not have the ability, assets or knowledge to take on a multimillion-dollar bridge project, the Obama plan will not help the average unemployed construction worker.

The same is true with highway construction. There are only a handful of grading and paving contractors in every state. When a government project comes up for bid, the executives will either place a low bid to acquire more work, or a higher bid when their schedules are full. Because most highway construction is accomplished using heavy equipment, there's very little opportunity for unemployed painters or electricians to acquire a job, unless of course, they want to direct traffic by waving an orange flag.

Even if President Obama's proposed $447 billion was actually used to fund federal construction projects, it would only be another job for those already established contractors—and it's very unlikely that the executives at these companies would hire any new employees. Unless Congress is willing to address the root cause of our problems, government stimulus would only provide temporary relief for a short period of time. The only viable long-term solution would be to address the decades-long trend of losing jobs to China.

As long as the majority of products that Americans buy come from China, we will have an ever-increasing problem with our economy driven by high unemployment. Almost all our large corporations have call centers located in the Philippines, India or any other country where labor is cheap. There was a time when Americans bought American-made products. When Americans buy American-made products, proceeds from those sales help to create jobs and allow our economy to thrive.

When companies like Wal-Mart started importing cheaper goods from China, customers started buying the lower-priced products. It didn't take long before the American-made manufacturing facilities closed their doors. Socks made in China are cheaper because the Chinese only pay their employees $4.50 per day. The Chinese are also able to produce cheaper products at the expense of pollution and other environmentally unsustainable practices. Instead of using higher-quality paint for our children's toys, many of these foreign companies would rather use lead-based paint in order to keep prices low.

When the American consumer was faced with this dilemma ten years ago, we had a choice to make: *Would we buy cheaper low-quality socks from China or high-quality socks from America?* Because the American consumer made the choice to buy foreign products, it forced many American manufacturing companies out of business. Because there are fewer manufacturing businesses left in America, we now have fewer jobs and a higher unemployment rate. When Americans can't find work, they can't pay their bills. When homeowners can't make their mortgage payments, it causes foreclosures, which in turn has a negative effect on the housing market.

The root cause of America's economic problems cannot be solved by more government stimulus. In fact, the more our government tries to stimulate the economy, the more our national debt increases, creating an even greater dependence on China, because they have become our banker. When intelligent business leaders hear about Obama's plans to stimulate the economy, it only frightens them more, causing them to pull back on any plans for expansion. Anyone with common sense can see the only way to solve America's economic problems is to bring our manufacturing jobs back to American soil.

Another aspect of our government's efforts to stimulate the economy that has frightened many financial experts around the world comes from the Federal Reserve Chairman Ben Bernanke's *QE* efforts. The term *quantitative easing* is used by the Federal Reserve to describe a technique that stimulates the economy by creating money out of thin air. The idea is that if banks had more money on their books, they may be more likely to loan more money to businesses and thus stimulate the economy.

The plan is to pump banks full of money so that they will loan the money to small businesses who will in turn build American-based manufacturing plants. To operate these new facilities, executives would need to hire employees. And thus, the unemployment rate will decrease and everything will go back to normal.

According to an article by *Bloomberg News* published on August 22, 2011, Federal Reserve Chairman Ben Bernanke's *unprecedented effort to keep the economy from plunging into depression included lending banks and other companies as much as $1.2 trillion of public money. The largest borrower, Morgan Stanley, got as much as $107.3 billion, while Citigroup took $99.5 billion and Bank of America $91.4 billion.*[3] The bailouts also included many European firms including Edinburgh-based Royal Bank of Scotland, which took $84.5 billion, and Zurich-based UBS, which got $77.2 billion.

After these banks received large sums of cash, their loan officers took a look at some possible lending options for American businesses. After studying the loan application for an American-based manufacturing plant, the bankers decided not to make the loan. They were concerned that no one would buy their higher-priced products and that the company could not compete with the cheaper imports from China.

After Ben Bernanke's first round of QE efforts failed to produce the desired results, he decided to lower the interest rate down to zero in hopes it would make it easier for American businesses to borrow money. The theory behind this is when American businesses borrow more money, they can build more factories and hire more employees, and thus, stimulate the economy. Now that the Federal Reserve has lowered the interest rate to zero and has promised to keep it at historically low rates for many years to come, some experts say Ben Bernanke may be running out of magic bullets.

The new round of quantitative easing, called *QE3*, comes from a strategy employed by Japan more then a decade ago. It didn't work very well for the Japanese economy, so there's little reason to believe that it will help the unemployment rate in America. QE3 works when the Federal Reserve offers to buy a bank's assets like government bonds. If the Federal Reserve offers a high enough price, the banks will agree to sell our government almost anything.

For example, let's say that Citigroup owns $90 billion in bonds. After negotiating a deal, the Federal Reserve will turn on the printing presses and create $100 billion to buy those bonds. Now that Citigroup has $100 billion in cash, the Federal Reserve is hoping they will loan that money to small business owners, who will in turn use the money to open up manufacturing facilities and hire more employees. So far, this strategy has not worked very well. The unemployment rate remains high, while the bankers (who created the sub-prime mortgage crisis), have only increased their own profits from the Federal Reserve's actions.

Another concern with the Federal Reserve's QE actions is that every time they turn on the printing presses (creating money from thin air), it devalues our hard-earned dollars and causes inflation. This is especially harmful for retired citizens who are living on fixed incomes. As inflation increases, so too does the cost of living. In the past few years, we have seen the price of food in grocery stores double. When the price of food, gas and rent doubles every five years, the amount of money within our seniors' retirement accounts may not be enough to last. Our elderly may run out of money and need to survive on more government subsidies.

The only way to effectively address the economic issues facing America would be to deal with the low-quality imports from China by imposing tariffs. If our federal government imposed a 30 percent import tax on every pair of socks from China, the high-quality American-made socks would be more attractive to customers. When shoppers went to Wal-Mart, they would have the choice to buy high-quality American-made wool socks for $2, or imported, synthetic fiber socks for $3.

Pretty soon, nobody in America would want to buy cheap Chinese products. American entrepreneurs would rush to their banks demanding construction loans to build manufacturing plants. Small business owners would need to hire tens of thousand of construction workers to build factories, and upon completion, they would need to hire hundreds of thousands more American workers to operate those businesses, and thus solve our economic problems.

This solution has already proved itself successful with tariffs imposed on Chinese tires. According to an article published by *The New York Times* on September 11, 2009, *The decision signals the first time that the United States has invoked a special safeguard provision that was part of its agreement to support China's entry into the World Trade Organization in 2001.*

Under that safeguard provision, American companies or workers harmed by imports from China can ask the government for protection simply by demonstrating that American producers have suffered a "market disruption" or a "surge" in imports from China.

American imports of Chinese tires tripled between 2004 and 2008, and China's share of the American market grew to 16.7 percent, from 4.7 percent, according to the United States Trade Representative. Four American tire factories closed in 2006 and 2007, and several more are set to close this year.

The International Trade Commission had already determined that Chinese tire imports were disrupting the $1.7 billion market and recommended that the president impose the new tariffs. Members of the commission, an independent government agency, voted 4-2 on June 29 to recommend that President Obama impose tariffs on Chinese tires for three years.[4]

Because the United States government already imposes a 4 percent tariff on Chinese tires, the new law would increase the tariff amount to 35 percent for the first year. The tariff amount would then be lowered to 30 percent the second year and 25 percent the third year. After that, the law expires and the tariff would go back to 4 percent. For the time being, this new law has saved the American-based tire manufacturing industry from going out of business.

The question is, Why wouldn't the Obama Administration impose higher and longer-term tariffs on all imported goods that have been harming American jobs? One possible explanation is that it would make Chinese business owners and Chinese government officials very angry. Some even say it could spark a trade war. If the Obama Administration imposed higher tariffs on all imported goods, Chinese officials might stop loaning the United States government money.

Because the Obama Administration wants to borrow more money to fund quick-fix solutions for our long-term problems, it is very unlikely that we will see any more tariffs against China. Once our 2016 Christ-in-Congress Presidential Team takes office, the American people will have a choice to make: Do you want to continue borrowing money from China to fund government stimulus, or do you want to impose higher tariffs on imported goods?

Do you want to live in a welfare state, or do you want to create a sustainable prosperous economy? With the 2016 Christ-in-Congress Campaign, you will have the opportunity to address these concerns through the public referendum platform.

CHAPTER SEVEN

AFFORDABLE HEALTH CARE WITHOUT TAXPAYER-FUNDED ABORTIONS

When President Obama sold his health care package to the nation, he said it would lower everybody's health insurance payments, plus reduce the federal deficit by diverting the growing cost of Medicare and Medicaid to other agencies. It sounded like a great plan at the time, although many experts were warning, *Anytime big government tries to take over private industry, disastrous results can be expected!*

A good example of these disastrous results is described in an article by the chairman of the House Committee on Oversight and Government Reform, which says, *Health care spending will increase because of Obamacare, according to a recent report from the Centers for Medicare and Medicaid Services. Premiums are set to increase for most Americans, and government actuaries now estimate the growth in the net cost of health insurance will increase by 14 percent—compared to 3.5 percent if Obamacare never passed.*

Now that the bill has passed, and experts have had an opportunity to analyze the law, it is becoming clear that Obamacare will be more expensive than advertised—adding to a deficit already crippling the economy.

So far, the main culprit is the law's expensive health insurance subsidies, available to some people who lack employer-sponsored health insurance. Beginning in 2014, tens of millions of employees will be eligible for these new subsidies. Many already have access to health insurance through their employers but are likely to find it more advantageous if this insurance is dropped, and they can instead have taxpayer health care subsidies and slightly higher wages.

While this creates a win-win for the employer and worker, it creates a lose-lose for the nation's credit rating and taxpayers. Obamacare, in fact, represents the largest expansion of the U.S. welfare state in nearly 50 years.

At a time when the nation's credit has been downgraded for the first time and our country is struggling to finance and reform existing entitlement programs, Obamacare's creation of new entitlements increases dependency on government and pushes our country deeper into a fiscal crisis of Greek proportion.[1]

Not only will the CR3590 Affordable Care Act add trillions of dollars to the U.S. deficit, but it has failed to address the underlying problems with our rising health care costs—namely, doctors who continue submitting higher and higher bills for their services.

A good example of rising health care costs comes from a man who visits his doctor and says, "I'm self-pay." Because the client is paying for the services in cash, the doctor's office will only charge the man $60 for an office visit. If the man has insurance, the doctor's office will submit a $240 bill to his insurance company for the same services.

When doctors are asked about this accounting discrepancy, most of them will say, *We have to submit $240 in hopes of being paid a fourth of that amount.* As this practice has grown over the years, it's understandable why some doctors would start submitting higher and higher bills to our insurance companies.

A good example of these over-inflated medical costs comes from a lawsuit filed against several physicians. According to an article published by *The Record* on March 25, 2011, *One of the nation's largest insurers has sued six North Jersey physicians over bills it considers "unlawful and excessive," including $56,980 for a 25-minute bedside consultation.*

In one case, Aetna Inc. claims it paid a Ridgewood neurosurgery practice $3.9 million more than it was entitled to receive. In another case, Aetna claims a cardiologist at Hackensack University Medical Center increased his charges more than six-fold for catheterizations, from $3,000 to $18,720.

The fees drove his income from Aetna up from $155,310 in 2006 to $2.5 million in 2008, according to the lawsuit obtained by The Record *on Thursday.*[2]

Now that the federal government has agreed to pay for everybody's health care, the medical industry will need oversight to prevent doctors from charging any amount they want for their services. One way to correct this problem would be to have an industry-wide standard of set prices for medical services. Another option would be for doctors to disclose the full amount for their services before they are rendered.

But even if hospitals disclosed the full cost of services before they were rendered, it would not prevent doctors from performing unnecessary services. The best way to provide this oversight would be through a patient's out-of-pocket expenses at the time the services are rendered. This method of checks-and-balances between consumers and service providers would be the best way to keep prices low and competitive.

A good analogy on how this would work comes from the automobile repair industry. Usually when a car breaks down, a conservative shopper will make a few telephone calls to inquire about prices. The usual response from a repair shop is, *We can't quote a price unless we see what's wrong with your car.* After the customer brings the car in for an estimate, there's usually room for negotiations. If the price is too high, the customer is free to take his car to a lower-priced shop.

Now imagine what would happen to the automobile industry if your mechanic could submit an unlimited amount of repair bills to the federal government for payment. Would your mechanic recommend a $20,000 overhaul? Or would he just rebuild the engine and install new brakes, then submit a $25,000 bill to your insurance company without your knowledge?

If the federal government agreed to pay for an unlimited amount of services, plus include a free rental car while the repairs were being made, you can imagine what would happen. Repair prices would skyrocket, mechanics would grow rich and the federal government would go broke. The only way to regulate an industry in this situation would be to make the customer pay for a percentage of the repairs himself. That way, the auto mechanic and the customer could discuss the need for a rebuilt engine, especially if the car was in good mechanical condition.

Low-income families who had to pay a large amount of medical bills during the year could receive a refund on their income tax returns, while higher-income families may only be allowed to claim a percentage of their out-of-pocket expense as a deduction. By incorporating these kinds of checks-and-balances into our health care system, we could provide high-quality coverage for all Americans, and at the same time keep prices low and competitive.

Another problem with the Affordable Care Act is the mandatory compliance clause that gives the Internal Revenue Service the authority to fine taxpayers if they don't have insurance. The current penalty is listed at $750, but it could be increased with future legislation.

The mandatory compliance clause is currently being challenged in the Supreme Court to see if the federal government has the right to force citizens to buy goods and services. If the mandate is upheld, it could give the federal government an unlimited amount of power. For example, let's say executives at an electric car company paid members of Congress billions of dollars in "consulting fees" to approve an Affordable Green Car Act.

If such a law were passed, it could require all Americans to buy electric cars. If anyone didn't want to buy an electric car, they could still drive around their old gas-guzzling vehicles, but they would have to pay a green car tax in the amount of $750 per year. If anybody refused to pay the penalty, the Internal Revenue

Service could employ any means necessary to collect the fees, including the confiscation of personal assets.

Another problem with the Affordable Care Act is that it uses taxpayer dollars to fund abortions. It also allows Planned Parenthood to operate in public schools and requires religious organizations such as Catholic hospitals, colleges, universities and other charitable organizations to provide birth control as part of their insurance coverage for employees.

According to a letter dated February 1, 2012, Most Reverend Michael J. Sheridan described the mandatory requirements as follows: *The U.S. Department of Health and Human Services announced last week that almost all employers, including Catholic employers, will be forced to offer their employees' health coverage that includes sterilization, abortion-inducing drugs, and contraception. Almost all health insurers will be forced to include those "services" in the health policies they write. And almost all individuals will be forced to buy that coverage as a part of their policies.*[3]

After conducting an extensive review of the Affordable Care Act, the National Right to Life Committee issued the following conclusion regarding abortions: *Buried deep in the Manager's Amendment was new language making a direct appropriation of funds for Community Health Centers (CHCs) (which are also called Federally Qualified Health Centers, or FQHCs), totaling $7 billion ($7,000,000,000).*

Because this is a direct appropriation in the health care bill itself, these funds will not flow through the annual appropriations bill for the Department of Health and Human Services. Therefore, these funds would not be covered by the Hyde Amendment.

The Hyde Amendment is a limitation provision that has been attached to the annual HHS appropriations bill in past years; this provision, so long as it is renewed annually, prevents the use of funds appropriated through that bill to pay for abortion or for plans that cover abortion, except to save the life of the mother, or in cases of rape and incest.[4]

Because there are no provisions in the Affordable Care Act to prevent federal taxpayer dollars from funding abortions, and because Community Health Centers are not obligated to operate under the Hyde Amendment, it means that all Community Health Centers are free to perform abortions using taxpayer dollars. The amount of funding for Community Health Care Centers is described in the Affordable Care Act as follows:[5]

CR 3590 Approved Funding
$700,000,000.00 for fiscal year 2011
$800,000,000.00 for fiscal year 2012
$1,000,000,000.00 for fiscal year 2013
$1,600,000,000.00 for fiscal year 2014
$2,900,000,000.00 for fiscal year 2015

In another review of the Affordable Care Act, a professor of law from the Catholic University of America made the following statement when asked if billions of dollars appropriated for Community Health Centers will be used to pay for abortions: *"It's not even a close question. Abortions will be covered. Without the Hyde Amendment, abortions not only may be covered, abortions must be covered."*[6]

From a Christian perspective, abortion is immoral for several reasons. The first reason is that God is the creator and sustainer of life. According to the book of Jeremiah, God says, *"Before I formed you in the womb I knew you, and before you were born I consecrated you."*[7]

The book of Psalms also acknowledges God as the creator and sustainer of life by saying, *For it was you who formed my inward parts; you knit me together in my mother's womb. My frame was not hidden from you, when I was being made in secret, intricately woven in the depths of the earth. Your eyes beheld my unformed substance. In your book were written all the days that were formed for me, when none of them as yet existed.*[8]

Because God is the creator of all life, and it is by God's Spirit that every living being is brought into existence, it is considered an offense against God to destroy what God is in the process of creating. The second reason why abortion is immoral is that it kills a child while harming the mother. *Women with a history of abortion have higher rates of anxiety (34% higher), depression (37%), alcohol use/misuse (110%), marijuana use (230%), and suicidal behavior (155%), compared to those who have not had an abortion.*[9]

All mothers have an inherent God-given desire to nurture and protect their children. We can see this protective quality in nature by observing a mother bear and her cubs. Ordinarily, a female bear will take every precaution necessary to avoid an encounter with a human, but when it comes time to protect her cubs, a mother bear will fight to the death. This inherent desire to protect her children comes from God, and it cannot be simply dismissed by making a choice to terminate a fetus.

This subconscious conflict develops deep inside a mother's heart when she has been given the responsibility to love, nurture and protect the life that is growing inside her, yet at the same time, fostering a desire to terminate that life. This conflict deep within her soul has the ability to surface years later in the form of anger, depression and even eating disorders.

The same situation occurs when soldiers go to war. Deep in every man's heart, God has written his law— thou shall not kill—yet a soldier has to follow orders. During the high stress of combat, many soldiers do not have the ability to process all these conflicting emotions, but several years later, many of our veterans return from war suffering nightmares, others with deep depression and guilty feelings to the point where it leads them to suicide. Many of our veterans have become consumed with drugs and alcohol and end up wandering the streets, homeless.

The same type of post-traumatic stress disorder surfaces in the lives of women many years after having an abortion. If in the event you have had an abortion, there's hope, healing and forgiveness available. Before you will be able to receive God's healing and restoration, it will be necessary to acknowledge your mistakes and accept the Lord's sacrifice on the cross for the forgiveness of your sins. Once you are restored to God's fellowship, you will have access to God's Spirit to go back into your past to heal any unresolved issues.

There are many loving, Christ-centered organizations available to help women work through the pain. Project Rachel Ministry would like to invite you to call their nationwide toll-free number, 888-456-HOPE

(4673), during regular business hours. You can also visit www.HopeAfterAbortion.com by clicking on the "Find Help" button to access a contact person nearest you.

If you are wondering what differences a pro-life president can make compared with a pro-choice president in regards to women's health issues, the National Right to Life foundation has provided the following information:[10]

Pro-Life	Pro-Choice
In 2003, President Bush signed into law the Partial-Birth Abortion Ban Act. When legal challenges were filed against the law, his administration successfully defended the law and it was upheld by the U.S. Supreme Court.	On his third day in office, President Obama nullified the pro-life "Mexico City Policy." By this action, President Obama made organizations that perform and promote abortion as a method of family planning eligible for U.S. foreign aid.
In 2007, President Bush sent congressional Democratic leaders letters in which he said that he would veto any bill that weakened any existing pro-life policy. This strong stance prevented successful attacks on the Hyde Amendment and many other pro-life laws during 2007 and 2008.	In March 2009, the Obama Administration announced that it would rescind (cancel) a conscience-protection regulation issued by the Bush Administration, which prevents the penalization of health care providers who refuse to participate in providing abortions.

Pro-Life	Pro-Choice
President Bush signed into law several other crucial pro-life measures, including the Unborn Victims of Violence Act, which recognizes unborn children as victims of violent federal crimes, the Born-Alive Infants Protection Act, which affords babies who survive abortions the same legal protections as babies who are spontaneously born prematurely.	In March 2009, President Obama issued an executive order that opened the door to federal funding of research that requires the killing of human embryos, reversing President Bush's 2001 order that blocked federal funding of embryo-killing research.
President Bush appointed two justices to the U.S. Supreme Court, Chief Justice John Roberts and Justice Samuel Alito. In 2007 both justices voted to uphold the federal Partial-Birth Abortion Ban Act.	President Obama has selected persons with extreme pro-abortion records for the top offices overseeing federal health programs, including Health and Human Services Secretary Kathleen Sebelius, former governor of Kansas, and Food and Drug Administration Commissioner Margaret Hamburg.

A few possible options for the American electorate to consider:

1. Prohibit Planned Parenthood from operating in public schools.

2. Amend the Affordable Care Act so that Community Health Centers will be subject to the terms of the Hyde Amendment.

3. Amend the Affordable Care Act by removing the requirement for religious-based organizations to provide birth control for their employees.

4. Limit the amount of abortions by restraining our sexually perverted culture with legislation that makes the distribution of pornography illegal.

5. Support the 2016 Christ-in-Congress Campaign so that the American people can vote on these issues through the referendum platform.

CHAPTER EIGHT

ESTABLISHING FOREIGN POLICY THAT TRANSFORMS THE WORLD

Nine days after a group of hijackers carried out an attack on the World Trade Center, President George W. Bush delivered a speech to Congress saying, *"The United States of America makes the following demands on the Taliban. Deliver to United States authorities all of the leaders of Al Qaeda who hide in your land.*

"Give the United States full access to terrorist training camps, so we can make sure they are no longer operating. These demands are not open to negotiation or discussion. The Taliban must act and act immediately. They will hand over the terrorists or they will share in their fate.

"Americans are asking, 'How will we fight and win this war?'

"We will direct every resource at our command—every means of diplomacy, every tool of intelligence, every instrument of law enforcement, every financial influence, and every necessary weapon of war—to the destruction and to the defeat of the global terror network.

"Now, this war will not be like the war against Iraq a decade ago, with a decisive liberation of territory and

a swift conclusion. It will not look like the air war above Kosovo two years ago, where no ground troops were used and not a single American was lost in combat.

"Our response involves far more than instant retaliation and isolated strikes. Americans should not expect one battle, but a lengthy campaign unlike any other we have ever seen. It may include dramatic strikes visible on TV and covert operations secret even in success.

"We will starve terrorists of funding, turn them one against another, drive them from place to place until there is no refuge or no rest. And we will pursue nations that provide aid or safe haven to terrorism. Every nation in every region now has a decision to make: Either you are with us or you are with the terrorists."[1]

In the months that followed, American forces invaded Iraq. Three years later, the pursuit of terrorists led us to invade Afghanistan, and on May 7, 2011, American forces invaded Pakistan on a raid to kill the Al Qaeda leader Osama bin Laden.

According to an article published by Reuters on June 29, 2011, the total cost for the wars in Iraq, Afghanistan and Pakistan will exceed $4 trillion ($4,000,000,000,000). When we divide $4 trillion by the number of people living in America, it comes to $13,300 per person. If a hardworking factory worker was married with three young children, he may be required to pay the U.S. Treasury $66,500 (5 x $13,300 per citizen = $66,500). An article from Reuters describes the cost of the war as follows:

The final bill will run at least $3.7 trillion and could reach as high as $4.4 trillion, according to the research *project "Costs of War" by Brown University's Watson Institute for International Studies.*

In the 10 years since U.S. troops went into Afghanistan to root out the Al Qaeda leaders behind the September 11, 2001, attacks, spending on the conflicts totaled $2.3 trillion to $2.7 trillion.

Those numbers will continue to soar when considering often overlooked costs such as long-term obligations to wounded veterans and projected war spending from 2012 through 2020. The estimates do not include at least $1 trillion more in interest payments coming due and many billions more in expenses that cannot be counted, according to the study.

In human terms, 224,000 to 258,000 people have died directly from warfare, including 125,000 civilians in Iraq. Many more have died indirectly, from the loss of clean drinking water, health care, and nutrition. An additional 365,000 have been wounded and 7.8 million people—equal to the combined population of Connecticut and Kentucky— have been displaced.

The report underlines the extent to which war will continue to stretch the U.S. federal budget, which is already on an unsustainable course due to an aging American population and skyrocketing health care costs. It also raises the question of what the United States gained from its multi-trillion-dollar investment. "I hope that when we look back, whenever this ends, something very good has come out of it," Senator Bob Corker, a Republican from Tennessee, told Reuters in Washington.[2]

Another cost associated with the wars in Iraq, Afghanistan and Pakistan is the damage it causes to

America's relationship with other Muslim countries. When citizens from Iraq have been interviewed, a common response has been, *We are happy you helped us overthrow an evil government dictator, but we do not want infidels in our country.*

The reason Muslims don't want foreign invaders in their country is understandable when we stop to consider our own feelings in the event an army invaded America. If someone from the door-to-door campaign asked every person on my block if they hated the Chinese so bad that they would pick up weapons to kill as many as possible, I'm sure everybody would answer, *No way! Killing is wrong! We don't want guns in our home. We love the Chinese people.*

How easy would it be to change my neighbor's mind if the Chinese army invaded America to help us get rid of all the corrupt politicians in Washington? At first my neighbor might say, *We are happy the Chinese helped us remove evil from Washington, but we don't want them in our country.*

If the Chinese army decided to set up camp and remain for the next five years, making raids on homes to search for what they called *terrorists,* I'm sure all kinds of allegations would surface. If the media started accusing the Chinese army of raping women and killing children, how hard would it be to incite the people who lived in my neighborhood to pick up automatic weapons to protect themselves? How hard would it be to stage a late-night attack on one of the foreign invaders' outposts?

The same situation has been occurring in Iraq and Afghanistan. In peaceful rural areas where no terrorists existed, the local men have been taking up arms, reporting for duty as soon as the infidel invaders entered their region. The longer American forces occupy Middle Eastern countries, the more hostility and hatred we create for ourselves.

A good example of the increased hostility that we are creating comes from the invasion of Pakistan. An article by the *Global Times* published on May 7, 2011, describes the increased hostility by saying, *Tensions are continuing between Pakistan and the U.S. resulting from the raid that killed Al Qaeda leader Osama bin Laden Monday in a compound near the capital, Islamabad.*

About 1,500 Pakistani Islamists took to the streets near the Pakistani city of Quetta on Friday, protesting against the killing of Bin Laden and saying that more figures like him would arise to wage holy war against the U.S., Reuters reported.

"Jihad (holy war) against America will not stop with the death of Osama," said Fazal Mohammad Baraich, a cleric, amid protestors shouting "Down with America" and burning American flags.

The protest came one day after a major Islamist party in Pakistan, Jamaat-e-Islami, called for mass protests against U.S. violation of Pakistan's sovereignty.

Islamabad reacted strongly after U.S. special forces killed Bin Laden early on Monday, as they claimed they were not informed of the operation in their territory. Pakistan's foreign secretary, Salman Bashir, warned Thursday of "disastrous consequences" if any other country staged an attack in its territory like the U.S. raid to kill Bin Laden.[3]

When more terrorists appear shouting hateful remarks, waving their machine guns, the more our American military steps up its efforts to eradicate them, creating even greater problems. Because Pakistan has nuclear weapons, the problems that we have just created will not be easy to solve without it costing the American taxpayer billions more in foreign aid.

According to an article published on February 23, 2010, *The Obama Administration in its latest annual budget has proposed $1.6 billion in military assistance and about $1.4 billion as civilian assistance to Pakistan.*[4] This takes the total aid to Pakistan to more than $20.7 billion since 9/11, according to data compiled from the Departments of Defense, Agriculture and the U.S. Agency for International Development.

From a worldly perspective, these events may seem very complex and difficult to solve, but when we look at the situation from a spiritual perspective, God has already given us the wisdom that we need: In the event of another terrorist attack, our first response should be to bond together, grieve our losses, restore, rebuild, learn valuable lessons and ultimately come to a place of peace and forgiveness. None of this will be possible without the necessary grace of God.

It's very common for people who have been hurt to seek justice. For most Americans, a desire for revenge comes from Hollywood movies. When an evil force attacks a nice family, everybody has a desire to hunt down the bad guys. In the movies, the good guys always win and the bad guys always lose, but it's not so simple in real life—especially when Sacred Scripture defines Satan as the ruler of this world.

Although the need to take revenge comes very naturally, it also creates greater problems in the future. After the attacks on the World Trade Center, Americans were outraged. Going to war seemed like a good idea. It's very easy for injured men to seek justice, except of course, if they had to pay for it in advance. Picture how our desire for war would have changed if President George W. Bush had made the following speech:

I want every man, woman and child living in America to send me a check in the amount of $13,300. If you are married with three young children living at home, you will need to send $66,500. Once we collect $4 trillion, we will engage in a ten-year-long war. A quarter of a million people will die, but in the end, we will finally get our man.

If faced with this proposal, I'm wondering how many Americans would want to consider some other options:

1. The first option for the American electorate to consider would be to expand programs at the United States Institute of Peace. Every year, this agency hosts an Annual Grant Competition where nonprofit corporations can submit their own peace-building plans for an award consideration. Priority Grants are currently available for countries like Pakistan, where the average award grant ranges between $45,000 to $140,000.[5]

The United States Institute of Peace also offers training seminars and workshops for those who are interested in becoming peace-builders. According to the USIP website, a variety of workshops are currently being offered such as "Stabilization and Peace-building."

This course is based on the lessons learned from international interventions and peace-building missions.[6]

Another possibility for the American electorate to consider would be to host peace-building seminars and workshops in every major city in America. Sending peace-building missionaries to Middle Eastern countries would have a better impact and lower cost than going to war. For the same amount that it cost to fight the wars in Iraq, Afghanistan and Pakistan, we could have sent 300 million short-term missionaries to every country in the world ($4 trillion ÷ 300,000,000 missionaries = $3,300 travel expense, plus $10,000 ministry allowance per person).

Three hundred million peace-building missionaries with $10,000 cash in their pockets could have purchased a vast quantity of rice to be giving away in poor villages. Peace-building missionaries could have also purchased seeds to grow crops and taken sick schoolchildren to the hospital. With the money that was left over, they could have bought the Imams and clerics a rich assortment of presents.

Because peace is a function of the heart, peace-building missionaries would have much better results at creating peace than spending $4 trillion in a ten-year war that has only seemed to create more problems. According to a quote from the United States Institute of Peace's website, *The more we sweat at peace, the less we bleed in war.*

2. Another option for the American electorate to consider would be to prohibit pornographic images from the public domain. When a majority of America's

enemies are interviewed, they commonly refer to America as the "Great Satan" because we are world's largest producer of pornographic material. In the event Congress passed new laws prohibiting the distribution of pornographic materials, it would go a long way toward establishing peace with our Muslim neighbors. It may even bring the Islamic "holy war" against America to an end.

3. Because the federal government cannot endorse, promote or fund any kind of religious activities, the following option for addressing the root cause behind Islamic terrorist activities would need to be accomplished by churches, private companies or nonprofit corporations. This option would allow peace-building missionaries the ability to address spiritual matters.

For example, the first lesson that could be introduced comes from the ninety-nine names of Allah. Some of Allah's names listed in the Koran are as follows:

Names of Allah	Surahs from the Koran
The Most Compassionate	(1:3) (17:110) (19:58) (21:112)
The Merciful	(2:163) (3:31) (4:100) (5:3) (5:98)
The Forgiving	(2:173) (8:69) (16:110) (41:32)
The Most Kind	(3:30) (9:117) (57:9) (59:10)
The Giver of Life	(3:156) (7:158) (15:23) (30:50)
The Loving One	(11:90) (85:14)
The Generous	(27:40) (82:6)
The Provider	(51:58)
The Bestower of Peace	(59:23)
The Source of All-Goodness	(52:28)

For Muslims, the names for Allah mentioned in the Koran reflect God's nature and character. Because Allah has chosen the path of being the most compassionate, merciful, bestower of peace, so too, should all of Allah's servants choose the same path. Because Allah has chosen the path of being loving and forgiving, so too, should all of his followers.

Another lesson that Messianic Muslims could share from the Koran concerns the Messiah. The Koran says eleven times that Jesus is the Messiah in the following Surahs: (3:45) (4:157) (4:171–172) (5:17) (5:72) (5:75) and (9:30–31). Because the word *messiah* in Aramaic means savior—the anointed one—the long awaited savior of the world, peace-building missionaries would have the opportunity to share how the Messiah has the ability to remove the barrier of sin that separates men from God's love.

Once the sinful barrier has been removed, peace-building missionaries could share how it would be possible for all men to be filled with the Holy Spirit. According to Surah 58:22, the Koran says, *As for such, He hath written faith upon their hearts and hath strengthened them with a Spirit from Him, and He will bring them into Gardens underneath which rivers flow, wherein they will abide.*[7] Once a man accepts the Messiah's sacrifice on the cross for the forgiveness of his sins, he can then pray to receive the gift of the Holy Spirit.

Once a man is filled with the Holy Spirit, God will start the internal conversion process necessary to change that person's life. Planting a small seed of the Holy Spirit into a man's heart is no different than planting a small seed into the heart of a nation's religion.

According to Mark 4:31–32, *It is like a mustard seed, which, when sown upon the ground, is the smallest of all the seeds on earth; yet when it is sown it grows up and becomes the greatest of all shrubs, and puts forth large branches, so that the birds of the air can make nests in its shade.*

Most people who live in impoverished, Third World countries only want to experience a better life. Maybe this is another reason why our enemies hate America. Most Americans live in luxury, while the majority of the world lives on less than $5 per day. If this were the case, another option for fighting terrorism would be for American peace-building missionaries to work together in partnership with other countries to bring about their own prosperity.

CHAPTER NINE

OUTLAWING PORNOGRAPHIC IMAGES FROM THE PUBLIC DOMAIN

According to an article by *60 Minutes, One of the biggest cultural changes in the United States over the past 25 years has been the widespread acceptance of sexually explicit material—pornography.*

In the space of a generation, a product that once was available in the back alleys of big cities has gone corporate, delivered now directly into homes and hotel rooms by some of the biggest companies in the United States.

It is estimated that Americans now spend somewhere around $10 billion a year on adult entertainment, which is as much as they spend attending professional sporting events, buying music or going out to the movies.[1]

Before the invention of television, home computers or the Internet, it would have been inconceivable for Americans to envision the day when their children could access pornographic images inside their own homes when left unattended for more than five minutes. Pornography has invaded the public domain to the point where families need to buy special filtration services to protect their schoolchildren from accidentally clicking on cleverly disguised links while doing their homework.

Because it is our government's responsibility to promote good social order, the 2016 Christ-in-Congress Presidential Team may need to take an aggressive stance against companies who disseminate pornography. From the Christian perspective, pornography is immoral because it portrays women (who have been created in the image and likeness of God) as mere sex objects. Pornography is also considered a capital sin, because it leads to more serious sins.

On the surface, pornography may seen like a harmless form of adult entertainment, but when a man watches a sexually explicit video, very subtle demonic spirits have the ability to enter his heart, causing a deeper desire for more sinful encounters. When a man commits any kind of sin, he is making an agreement with evil. He is saying *no* to God's laws and *yes* to some kind of fleshly desire. When unconfessed sins develop a stronghold within a man's heart, they will eventually cause him to lose a desire for prayer. Men with unconfessed sins on their soul may even start making excuses for not attending church on Sunday.

When his family is attending church without him, those very subtle spirits will start calling him back for another video. After experiencing a difficult day at the office, he may start looking for comfort on the Internet, instead of turning to God in prayer. Eventually, he will find himself being drawn back to more sexually explicit material in an attempt to make himself feel better. Pretty soon, what started out as a harmless form of adult entertainment has turned into a full-blown addiction.

When his wife finds out, she will no longer feel like the love of his life. Communication within the marriage may eventually break down. Fighting over small issues may escalate. As the man's marriage suffers, the seductive sin of lust, backed by the power of the demonic, has the ability to drive the man into the arms of a prostitute for comfort. When his wife finds out that he has been sleeping around (or has contracted AIDS), their marriage could end in divorce—their children's lives in devastation.

If in the event you have found yourself addicted to pornography, there's hope and healing available for you. You will be able to find healing and accountability through your local church. The following ministries also offer resources to break the bonds of a pornography addiction:

Christian Websites	Description
www.pornharms.com	Morality In Media
www.focusonthefamily.com	Focus on the Family
www.settingcaptivesfree.com	Setting Captives Free
www.freedomeveryday.org	Life Ministries International
Catholic Websites	Description
www.chastity.com	Theology of the Body
www.unityrestored.com	Alpha Omega Clinic
www.maritalhealing.com	Institute for Marital Healing
www.catholictherapists.com	Find a Catholic therapist
www.familylifecenter.net	Family Life Center International
Secular Websites	Description
Socialcostsofpornography.com	The social costs of pornography

As sexually explicit material continues to invade our culture, high school students are being led to believe that sex is good for everyday recreation. When their parents are not around, teenage boys have been spending time watching porn on television and downloading videos from the Internet. When our young men enter into dating relationships, they want to act on these sexual urges, which eventually leads to their girlfriends' unwanted pregnancies. Our current government's response to this problem has been providing free condoms to high school students and abortions for young girls, all at the taxpayer's expense.

All this may make perfect sense from a worldly perspective; the more sexually perverted America becomes, the more America will need free birth control and taxpayer-funded abortions. But from a spiritual perspective, it would make more sense to outlaw all forms of sexually explicit material from the public domain and thereby save taxpayers billions of dollars. This approach would also protect our young girls from experiencing the trauma incurred by an abortion procedure.

Another reason why our 2016 Christ-in-Congress Presidential Team should take an aggressive stance against pornography is the damage it causes our relationships with Middle Eastern countries. When the majority of America's enemies are interviewed, the typical response has been *America the Great Satan— producer of pornography.* Eventually, those who harbor anti-American attitudes form terrorist groups and plan attacks on American soil. When terrorist strikes occur, our government's response has been to spend $4 trillion hunting down a handful of religious fanatics who are intent on teaching America a lesson about holiness.

Instead of spending another $4 trillion trying to chase down whoever takes Osama bin Laden's place, maybe a better option would be to remove the pornographic filth from American's public domain—to make the distribution of sexually explicit images on television, the Internet and in magazines illegal. That way we could end the Islamic "holy war" on terror, reduce the number of abortions and spend less government money handing out free condoms to schoolchildren.

As you can imagine, a law that would require the removal of all pornographic images from the public domain would cause the entire sex-trade to rise up in protest. Porn producers would send lobbyists to buy as many votes from Congress as possible. There would be allegations that the new law violated the sex-trade's First Amendment rights—that it hindered their right to freedom of speech and the press. Heavy-litigation lawyers would pursue the case all the way to the Supreme Court.

When the *Sex Trade Industry vs. United States Government* case comes before the Supreme Court, the pornography industry would cite the First Amendment by saying, *Congress shall make no law respecting an establishment of religion, or prohibiting the free exercise thereof; or abridging the freedom of speech, or of the press; or the right of the people peaceably to assemble, and to petition the Government for a redress of grievances.*[2]

Attorneys for the pornography industry would argue that they have freedom of speech to say anything they want, the freedom of expression to broadcast anything they want, and the freedom of press to print anything they want. They may even claim that pornography was part of their religious worship, thus protected under religious freedom.

In another case involving the interpretation of the Constitution (*Reynolds vs. United States*), the defendant was accused of practicing bigamy in the territory of Utah. Apparently, Reynolds had more than one wife and claimed bigamy was part of his religious beliefs. For his defense, Reynolds used many religious arguments from the Bible by referencing King Solomon, who had more than 700 wives. Reynolds also presented arguments that the Ten Commandments did not condemn the practice of bigamy, nor was the prohibition of bigamy mentioned in the New Testament.

Muslims living in America could make the same argument. According to the Koran, Muslims can have up to four wives, providing that they can financially afford them. In the same way, Reynolds argued that the practice of bigamy was part of his religion and that the federal government could not hinder his religious freedom—that his religious freedom was protected under the First Amendment.

When the court studied the case, it went back to see what our Founding Fathers intended by freedom of religion. What they discovered was that the government could *not* use its power to influence a man's opinions about religion, but that our government was free to create laws that protected well-being and good order within society. The court concluded *that to make religious rule of law superior to civil law would make each person "law unto himself" and render the government ineffectual and irrelevant.*[3]

In the Reynolds case, the federal government could not influence the man's religious beliefs, but our government has jurisdiction over its citizen's actions. When the Supreme Court reviews the Sex Trade Industry case, the justices may need to go back and study what our Founding Fathers meant by abridging the freedom of speech or of the press. Does it mean that Americans are free to share their personal opinions in written and printed form without government censorship? Or does it give men the right to defile the public domain with pornographic images?

Consenting adults are free to do (almost anything) they want in the privacy of their own homes, but once their actions enter into the public domain, the government has a right of censorship. Criminal cases concerning indecent exposure are a good example of our government's right to enforce such laws. Sexual predators may want to interpret the First Amendment's freedom of expression giving them the right to express themselves any way they want. But when a man in a trench coat goes into a public building and starts flashing young children, he can be arrested and brought to trial. When found guilty, he could face time in jail as well as having to register as a sex offender.

If the 2016 Christ-in-Congress Presidential Team had the opportunity to nominate several justices to the Supreme Court, the pornography case could very easily be decided on our government's behalf. In the event the Supreme Court found that the sex trade had the right to invade the public domain with pornographic images according to their First Amendment rights, another option would be to amend the Constitution.

There was a time in American history when the Constitution of the United States prohibited the consumption of alcohol. After the Civil War, gambling, prostitution and public drunkenness was on the rampage. In an effort to combat the immoral darkness that had swept across our nation, the Anti-Saloon League was established in 1893. Their mission was to outlaw intoxicating liquors.

The Anti-Saloon League first started polling political candidates about their views on alcohol consumption. In the 1915 elections, a majority of Anti-Saloon candidates took control of Congress, and on December 18, 1917, Congress passed the 18th Amendment prohibiting the sale and consumption of alcohol in the United States. Although the law remained in effect for more than twenty years, it did not stop the illegal production of moonshine.

Because the sale of alcohol was viewed as a good source of revenue for the national and local governments, along with a growing movement to elect "wet" candidates to Congress, the 18th Amendment was repealed and replaced by the 21st Amendment on December 5, 1933, making the sale and consumption of alcohol legal in the United States.

Regardless of the actions our 2016 Christ-in-Congress Presidential Teams takes, the pornography industry will not simply cease and desist without a major battle. If Christians do nothing but attend church on Sunday, the world will continue growing more and more evil. A sexually perverted, demonic-influenced culture will emerge, unless a few good men take a stand. The battle over our public domain will be fierce, but the rewards and victory will be worth the effort.

God has blessed America with the precious gift of freedom. You can use your freedom right now to support the 2016 Christ-in-Congress Campaign.

CHAPTER TEN

UPHOLDING OUR NATION'S ETHICS, VALUES AND MORALS

The 2016 Christ-in-Congress Campaign represents more than just the removal of corrupt politicians from Washington. The complete vision includes the establishment and enforcement of laws that reflect our nation's ethics, values and morals. A good example of the attack on our nation's ethics comes from the growing number of medical marijuana dispensaries that have swept across the country.

Ever since the Obama Administration issued a statement saying they would *not* enforce federal drug laws, thousands of medical marijuana dispensaries have appeared. An article published by the Associated Press on October 19, 2009, describes the situation as follows: *The Obama Administration will not seek to arrest medical marijuana users and suppliers as long as they conform to state laws, under new policy guidelines to be sent to federal prosecutors Monday.*

Two Justice Department officials described the new policy to The Associated Press, saying prosecutors will be told it is not a good use of their time to arrest people who use or provide medical marijuana in strict compliance with state laws. The new policy is a significant departure from the Bush administration, which insisted it would continue to enforce federal anti-pot laws regardless of state codes.

Fourteen states allow some use of marijuana for medical purposes: Alaska, California, Colorado, Hawaii, Maine, Maryland, Michigan, Montana, Nevada, New Mexico, Oregon, Rhode Island, Vermont and Washington. California is unique among those for the widespread presence of dispensaries—businesses that sell marijuana and even advertise their services.

Colorado also has several dispensaries, and Rhode Island and New Mexico are in the process of licensing providers, according to the Marijuana Policy Project, a group that promotes the decriminalization of marijuana use.

Attorney General Eric Holder said in March that he wanted federal law enforcement officials to pursue those who violate both federal and state law, but it has not been clear how that goal would be put into practice.[1]

If you are wondering why the Obama Administration doesn't want to enforce federal drug laws, some liberals say it's part of his social agenda. Others speculate that if the Obama Administration can get the vast majority of Americans addicted to medical marijuana and other pharmaceutical drugs, there would be fewer people to oppose his Domestic Partners Benefits and Obligations Act, homosexual hate-crime laws and other gay agendas.

An article published by *The Los Angeles Times* on June 30, 2009, describes President Obama's homosexual agenda as follows: *Facing a political backlash from an important voting bloc, President Obama met with leaders of the gay and lesbian community Monday, asking for patience and assuring them that in time he will usher in policy changes that protect them from discriminatory treatment.*

"We've been in office six months now," the president said. "I suspect that by the time this administration is over, I think you guys will have pretty good feelings about the Obama Administration."

Some in attendance applauded Obama for assembling such a large group of gay and lesbian leaders in the White House. "The very fact that he would invite 200 LGBT [lesbian, gay, bisexual, transgender] leaders from across the nation on the 40th anniversary of the beginning of the gay liberation movement is just an astounding thing," said Bishop V. Gene Robinson, who is gay.

"Most people were standing around not believing they were actually guests in the White House. He expressed his opposition to the same things that we're all opposed to, and his support for things we hope to see happen: the end of 'don't ask, don't tell,' employment nondiscrimination and the overturning of the Defense of Marriage Act."[2]

During this meeting, President Obama made numerous promises to the gay community, including the repeal of the Don't Ask, Don't Tell policy that he signed into law on December 22, 2010. During this meeting, President Obama also made many other promises by saying, *"I'm also urging Congress to pass the Domestic Partners Benefits and Obligations Act, which will guarantee the full range of benefits, including health care, to LGBT couples and their children."[3]*

President Obama also said, *"My administration is*

also working hard to pass an employee non-discrimination bill and hate-crimes bill, and we're making progress on both fronts."[4]

All of these promises may sound very good if you are a member of the LGBT movement, but what effect will these proposed new laws have on the 76 percent of Christians living in America? On the surface, hate-crime laws sound very good. When we think about hate-crimes against homosexuals, most Americans would envision a group of angry protestors calling a gay couple names, holding signs and making threats of violence.

If this were the case, these actions are already illegal in America. We already have existing laws protecting citizens against assault, harassment and threats. Anyone who violates our existing laws can be arrested, brought to trial and, if found guilty, sentenced to jail. Even if a homosexual couple experienced a domestic dispute and one of them started acting in this manner toward his lover, the person who was being harassed could call the police and obtain a restraining order.

The kind of anti-discriminatory laws that President Obama is proposing already exist in several other countries, and the results have been less than favorable for Christians. Once an anti-discriminatory law for homosexuals takes effect, a gay man can show up for a job interview and start talking about this sex life. If in the event the man was not awarded the job, he could sue the business based on grounds of sexual-preference discrimination.

After Sweden passed a hate-crime law, a Pentecostal pastor named Ake Green was arrested and brought to trial for preaching a sermon about homosexuality. According to an article published on October 2, 2004, *He was convicted in July of "hate speech" against homosexuals. His views were strongly and publicly expressed in a sermon.*

He preached that homosexuality is "abnormal, a horrible cancerous tumor in the body of society," and he supported this view with Bible verses. Pastor Green was charged with "inciting hatred," and went on trial in June.[5] After Pastor Green received a thirty-day jail sentence for preaching God's Word, he appealed his case to the Swedish Supreme Court, which cleared him of the charges.

The same kind of homosexual hate-crime laws have also passed in Canada. According to an article published on April 29, 2004, *LifeSiteNews.com was informed by the Governor General's office today that homosexual hate-crime Bill C-250 was given Royal Assent this morning, putting the law into effect.*

The Evangelical Fellowship of Canada (EFC) said it was deeply disturbed at the passage of the bill and the possible impact on religious freedom in Canada. Bill C-250, a private members bill, includes the phrase "sexual orientation" in the groups protected against the spread of hate propaganda in the Criminal Code.

The Senate passed the bill yesterday despite an outpouring of concern from hundreds of thousands of Canadians. Dr. Janet Epp Buckingham, director of Law and Public Policy of the EFC, said, "This legislation comes at a time when issues of sexual morality and marriage are at the forefront of public debate. Without a clear definition of

what is criminal hatred, it is ambiguous what public state-
ments will be considered criminal."[6]

According to the new Canadian law, if anyone
makes a public statement in regard to what the Bible
teaches about homosexuality, that person could be
found guilty of a criminal offense. Because church
services are considered to be within the public domain,
the pastor's sermon may be subject to government
censorship. Not only does the new Canadian law apply
to hate-crime speech, but it also applies to God's written Word.

On December 11, 2002, a judgment was entered
against a man (*Owens vs. Saskatchewan*) for placing
an advertisement in the local newspaper for anti-
homosexual bumper stickers. The advertisement is
described by court documents as follows: *The bumper
sticker in the advertisement displayed references to four
Bible passages: Romans 1, Leviticus 18:22, Leviticus 20:13
and 1 Corinthians 6:9–10, on the left side of the sticker.
An equal sign (=) was situated in the middle of the sticker,
with a symbol on the right side of the sticker. The symbol
on the right side was comprised of two males holding
hands with the universal symbol of a red circle with a
diagonal bar superimposed over top.*[7]

It was the court's responsibility to determine if the
bumper stickers with four Bible verses and two stick
figures of gay men holding hands violated the law that
reads as follows: *No person shall publish or display, or
cause or permit to be published or displayed, on any lands
or premises or in a newspaper, through a television or radio
broadcasting station or any other broadcasting device, or
in any printed matter or publication or by means of any*

other medium that he owns, controls, distributes or sells, any representation, including without restricting the generality of the foregoing, any notice, sign, symbol, emblem, article, statement or other representation:

(A) Which exposes, or tends to expose, to hatred, ridicules, belittles or otherwise affronts the dignity of any person, any class of persons or a group of persons; because of his or their race, creed, religion, colour, sex, sexual orientation, family status, marital status, disability, age, nationality, ancestry, place of origin or receipt of public assistance.[8]

The court's findings are described as follows: *The Board found that the advertisement of the bumper stickers exposed the complainants to hatred, ridicule and an affront to their dignity because of their sexual orientation contrary to this section.*[9]

When Owens appealed for a higher court to review his case, the same decision was rendered: *Having reviewed all of the evidence, the Board accepts that the universal symbol for forbidden, not allowed or not wanted, consisting of a circle with a slash through it, may itself not communicate hatred. However, when combined with the passages from the Bible, the Board finds that the advertisement would expose or tend to expose homosexuals to hatred or ridicule, or may otherwise affront their dignity on the basis of their sexual orientation. It is a combination of both the symbol and the biblical references which have led to this conclusion.*[10]

With the approval of these new hate-crime laws in Canada, homosexuals now have the ability to go around looking for Christians to persecute. If a man has a Bible verse on his car (Leviticus 20:13) that constitutes hatred toward homosexuals, he could be found guilty of a criminal offense and end up in jail. If a pastor preaches a message from the Bible concerning God's purpose for sexuality, he may also be convicted of a hate-crime against homosexuals and end up in prison.

The verse used in the Canadian court comes from Leviticus 20:13, which says, *If a man lies with a male as with a woman, both of them have committed an abomination; they shall be put to death; their blood is upon them.* The Bible also prescribes the death penalty for a number of other sins including adultery as per Leviticus 20:10, which says, *If a man commits adultery with the wife of his neighbor, both the adulterer and the adulteress shall be put to death.*

The death penalty was prescribed for the Levitical priesthood more than 3,500 years ago as a way to purge evil from society. From a spiritual perspective, the penalty for all sin is death. When a man committed a sin in the Old Testament, he either had to pay the death penalty himself, or he had to place the death penalty upon a sacrificial lamb. After the lamb had been sacrificed, blood from the lamb atoned for the man's sins.

In the New Testament, God sent his only begotten Son to take the place of the sacrificial lamb. Because God's laws never change, the penalty for sin is still death. When a man commits any kind of sin, the penalty of death takes the form of eternal separation from God. Because all men have sinned and fallen short, all men have a choice to make: We can pay the death penalty ourselves, or we can ask Jesus, the sacrificial lamb of God, to pay the death penalty on our behalf.

From the Christian perspective, gay, lesbian, bisexual and transgender members of society should not be stoned to death or hated; rather, they should acknowledge that the sin of homosexuality is an offense against God's plan for conjugal love between a married man and woman. They should also recognize that the penalty for all sin is death and make a choice to choose Jesus as Savior. Once their sins have been forgiven, they can ask to receive the gift of the Holy Spirit to help them heal any childhood wounds that may be contributing to their homosexual tendencies.

A good example of the childhood wounds that contribute to homosexual tendencies comes from a man named Jim. After attending church for several years, Jim was having a difficult time trying to break free from his homosexual disposition. When a Christian counselor associated with the 2016 Christ-in-Congress Campaign first met Jim, they prayed together and asked the Holy Spirit to shine the light of truth deep into Jim's heart to illuminate any childhood wounds that may be contributing to his tendencies.

The first issue that was discovered was Jim's father, who spent most of his time away from the family home. The absence of Jim's father during his early childhood caused him to experience a deep subconscious desire for his father's love. Jim needed to be loved by his father, yet his father was never around. These unfulfilled needs developed into a hunger to receive love and attention from men later on in his life.

To make matters worse, Jim's mother was oftentimes abusive, which caused him to resent women. The Holy Spirit also brought to mind all the times when

Jim was teased and picked on by girls in his elementary school. The combination of his resentment toward women, plus a deep subconscious desire to be loved by men, were driving forces behind Jim's homosexual tendencies.

Before Jim could break free, he needed to go back into his past and work through his emotional wounds. Jim needed to forgive his mother for all the abuse and shameful things she did to him. Jim also needed to forgive his father for not being able to provide the love, encouragement and support that he needed. After Jim forgave his parents, he asked the Holy Spirit to take the place of hurt within his heart. After completing his emotional healing work, Jim's homosexual desires completely disappeared.

If in the event you are struggling with homosexual tendencies, there's hope and healing available for you. The following ministries are available to help you break the addiction cycle so that you may experience the fullness of your heavenly Father's love:

Ministry Websites	Description
www.exodusinternational.org	Exodus International
www.christians-in-recovery.org	Christians in Recovery
www.christianhealingmin.org	Christian Healing Ministries
www.comingoutstraight.com	International Healing Foundation
www.christianrecovery.com	Christian Recovery International

Another issue that prevents homosexuals from breaking free is a belief that they were created by God to be gay, or that they evolved from nature with homosexual tendencies. From the Christian perspective, we know that God is the author of life and that God's Spirit brings all living beings to life. Because God is the author, creator and sustainer of all life, he would not create humanity with homosexual tendencies and at the same time declare those actions sinful.

From the viewpoint of every major world religion, homosexuality is considered to be gravely contrary to God's laws and to the laws of nature. According to the Jewish Torah, God gave the command: *Thou shalt not lie with mankind, as with womankind; it is abomination.*[11]

According to the book of Romans: *For this reason God gave them up to degrading passions. Their women exchanged natural intercourse for unnatural, and in the same way also the men, giving up natural intercourse with women, were consumed with passion for one another. Men committed shameless acts with men and received in their own persons the due penalty for their error.*

And since they did not see fit to acknowledge God, God gave them up to a debased mind and to things that should not be done. They were filled with every kind of wickedness, evil, covetousness, malice. Full of envy, murder, strife, deceit, craftiness, they are gossips, slanderers, God-haters, insolent, haughty, boastful, inventors of evil, rebellious toward parents, foolish, faithless, heartless, ruthless. They know God's decree, that those who practice such things deserve to die—yet they not only do them but even applaud others who practice them.[12]

The Catechism of the Catholic Church also says, *Basing itself on Sacred Scripture, which presents homosexual acts as acts of grave depravity, tradition has always*

declared that homosexual acts are intrinsically disordered.
They are contrary to the natural law. They close the sexual
act to the gift of life. They do not proceed from a genuine
affective and sexual complementarity. Under no circum-
stances can they be approved.[13]

In addition to the fact that all major religions condemn homosexuality, Sacred Scripture also instructs Christians to proclaim God's truth to all generations. Christians are required to proclaim God's Word to all nations so that all men can come to the saving knowledge of our Lord, Jesus Christ. At the opposite extreme, members of the LGBT movement want to condemn the Bible as hate literature, and they have been very successful getting liberal governments to rule in their favor.

From the spiritual perspective, this battle has been raging since the dawn of creation—it's a battle between good and evil. The homosexual movement wants to promote their values inside every public school in America. They want to teach young boys how to have sex with each other, and for young girls to do the same.

Even if members of the LGBT movement were allowed inside public schools to teach our children, it would not be enough. They would continue protesting for more rights. They would not stop until the Bible had been condemned as hate literature. Once the Obama homosexual hate-crime laws take effect, the LGBT movement will protest for all forms of prayer to be abolished. Eventually they would want to outlaw the concept of God, because after all, it was God who condemned their homosexual behaviors in the first place.

In the event you do not like the direction our nation is heading, you have the opportunity to do something about it right now. Your country needs you to take action immediately! Schoolchildren need your protection. Teenagers who are being offered medical marijuana need you to take a stand for righteousness.

We need your help to conduct a nationwide, door-to-door evangelization program. We need volunteers to make the 2016 Christ-in-Congress Campaign successful. Religious freedom needs your financial support!

Please take action immediately.

APPENDIX ONE

OUR FOUNDING FATHERS' RELIGION

The following list contains the names of the Founding Fathers that signed the Declaration of Independence along with their religious affiliations.[1] The majority of these men were devout in their faith and solid in their biblically based ethics, values and morals. They made great sacrifices for the freedom that we experience today.

State	Signer's Name	Affiliation
Connecticut	Samuel Huntington	Congregationalist
Connecticut	Roger Sherman	Congregationalist
Connecticut	William Williams	Congregationalist
Connecticut	Oliver Wolcott	Congregationalist
Delaware	George Read	Episcopalian
Delaware	Caesar Rodney	Episcopalian
Delaware	Thomas McKean	Presbyterian
Georgia	Lyman Hall	Congregationalist
Georgia	George Walton	Episcopalian
Georgia	Button Gwinnett	Episcopalian/Congregationalist
Maryland	Charles Carroll	Catholic
Maryland	Samuel Chase	Episcopalian
Maryland	William Paca	Episcopalian
Maryland	Thomas Stone	Episcopalian
Massachusetts	Samuel Adams	Congregationalist
Massachusetts	John Hancock	Congregationalist

State	Signer's Name	Affiliation
Massachusetts	John Adams	Congregationalist/ Unitarian
Massachusetts	Robert Treat Paine	Congregationalist/ Unitarian
Massachusetts	Elbridge Gerry	Episcopalian
New Hampshire	Josiah Bartlett	Congregationalist
New Hampshire	William Whipple	Congregationalist
New Hampshire	Matthew Thornton	Presbyterian
New Jersey	Francis Hopkinson	Episcopalian
New Jersey	Abraham Clark	Presbyterian
New Jersey	John Hart	Presbyterian
New Jersey	Richard Stockton	Presbyterian
New Jersey	John Witherspoon	Presbyterian
New York	Francis Lewis	Episcopalian
New York	Lewis Morris	Episcopalian
New York	William Floyd	Presbyterian
New York	Philip Livingston	Presbyterian
North Carolina	John Penn	Episcopalian
North Carolina	William Hooper	Episcopalian
North Carolina	Joseph Hewes	Quaker/Episcopalian
Pennsylvania	George Ross	Episcopalian
Pennsylvania	Robert Morris	Episcopalian
Pennsylvania	John Morton	Episcopalian
Pennsylvania	Benjamin Franklin	Episcopalian/Deist
Pennsylvania	James Wilson	Episcopalian/Presbyterian

State	Signer's Name	Affiliation
Pennsylvania	George Clymer	Quaker/Episcopalian
Pennsylvania	James Smith	Presbyterian
Pennsylvania	George Taylor	Presbyterian
Pennsylvania	Benjamin Rush	Presbyterian
Rhode Island	William Ellery	Congregationalist
Rhode Island	Stephen Hopkins	Episcopalian
South Carolina	Thomas Heyward Jr.	Episcopalian
South Carolina	Thomas Lynch Jr.	Episcopalian
South Carolina	Arthur Middleton	Episcopalian
South Carolina	Edward Rutledge	Episcopalian
Virginia	Francis Lightfoot Lee	Episcopalian
Virginia	Richard Henry Lee	Episcopalian
Virginia	Carter Braxton	Episcopalian
Virginia	Benjamin Harrison	Episcopalian
Virginia	Thomas Nelson Jr.	Episcopalian
Virginia	George Wythe	Episcopalian
Virginia	Thomas Jefferson	Episcopalian/Deist

501(C)(3) TAX-EXEMPT STATUS

According to the Internal Revenue Service, churches that operate under a 501(c)(3) status cannot get involved with politics. They are *prohibited from directly or indirectly participating in, or intervening in, any political campaign on behalf of (or in opposition to) any candidate for elective public office. Violation of this prohibition may result in denial or revocation of tax-exempt status and the imposition of certain excise tax.*[1]

The rules governing nonprofit organizations are not intended to *restrict free expression on political matters by leaders of churches or religious organizations speaking for themselves, as individuals. Nor are leaders prohibited from speaking about important issues of public policy. However, for their organizations to remain tax exempt under IRC section 501(c)(3), religious leaders cannot make partisan comments in official organization publications or at official church functions.*[2]

Because of these regulations, the best way for church officials to be involved with the 2016 Christ-in-Congress Campaign would be to keep their church's name and religious affiliation separate from their voter education efforts. For example, according to IRS publication 1828, *Tax guide for Churches and Religious Organizations, 501(c)(3) organizations are permitted to conduct certain voter education activities (including the presentation of public forums and the publication of voter education guides) if they are carried out in a non-partisan manner. In addition, section 501(c)(3) organizations may encourage people to participate in the electoral process through voter registration and get-out-the-vote drives, conducted in a non-partisan manner.[3]*

In the event that a church pays their employees to operate a voter registration booth and advertises their church's name and service times on the booth, their employees are not allowed to discuss politics with the general public. In the event the operators of that booth want to discuss religion and politics, they would need to display the Christ-in-Congress Campaign's name on the booth and pay for the event using private funds. That way the individual citizens operating the booth (who just happen to attend church on Sunday) could discuss anything they wanted with the general public without risking their church's 501(c)(3) status.

Another option for concerned citizens to consider would be to rent a room at the public library for the purpose of conducting a town hall meeting. If hundreds of people were expected, larger meeting halls may be available at the county fairgrounds or other government facilities. Once the general public had gathered, it would then be possible to organize a door-to-door evangelization program and voter registration tables in every shopping mall, grocery store and parking lot across their district.

For more information on how to protect your church's 501(c)(3) status while at the same time evangelizing America, please review IRS publication 1828, *Tax Guide for Churches and Religious Organizations.*

OUR ELECTORAL COLLEGE SYSTEM

Our electoral college system works by assigning each state a number of presidential votes that reflects the number of senators and house representatives that it sends to Congress. A total of 538 votes are available within the United States, and it only takes 270 to win the presidential election.

If the 2016 Christ-in-Congress Campaign received 51 percent of the votes in the top eleven states, our Presidential Team would win the election. The top eleven states would produce 270 electoral votes as follows: California (55), Texas (38), New York (29), Florida (29), Pennsylvania (20), Illinois (20), Ohio (18), Michigan (16), Georgia (16), North Carolina (15) and New Jersey (14).

NOTES

Unless otherwise noted, the following sources are cited under Title 17 U.S.C. Section 107 for informational, research and educational purposes. They are not affiliated with the Christ-in-Congress Campaign nor have they endorsed any products, services or content herein.

Chapter One
How Will We Pay for This?

1. One Hundred Tenth Congress, "Text of H.R. 5140 [110th]: Economic Stimulus Act of 2008," Govtrack.us (February 8, 2008): http://www.govtrack.us/congress/billtext.xpd?bill=h110-5140.

2. Greg Hitt and Deborah Solomon, "Historic Bailout Passes as Economy Slips Further," *The Wall Street Journal* (October 4, 2008): http://online.wsj.com/article/SB122304922742602533.html.

3. Laura Meckler, "Obama Signs Stimulus into Law," *The Wall Street Journal* (February 18, 2009): http://online.wsj.com/article/SB123487951033799545.html.

4. Karen Yourish and Laura Stanton, "Breaking Down Obama's Jobs Plan," *The Washington Post* (September 8, 2011): http://www.washingtonpost.com/business/economy/breaking-down-obamas-jobs-plan/2011/09/08/gIQAaZpEDK_graphic.html.

5. Margaret Chadbourn, "Obama to Ask for Debt Limit Hike: Treasury Official," Reuters (December 27, 2011): http://www.reuters.com/article/2011/12/27/us-usa-treasury-debt-idUSTRE7BQ0KU20111227.

Chapter Two
Vote for Me and Everything Will Be Free

1. Peter Valdes-Dapena, "Clunkers: Taxpayers Paid $24,000 Per Car," CNNMoney.com (October 29, 2009): http://money.cnn.com/2009/10/28/autos/clunkers_analysis/index.htm. From CNNMoney, October 29, 2009 © 2009 Time Inc. Used under license. CNNMoney and Time Inc. are not affiliated with, and do not endorse products or services of, Licensee.

2. Edmunds.com press release, "Cash for Clunkers Results Finally In: Taxpayers Paid $24,000 per Vehicle Sold, Reports Edmunds.com," (October 28, 2009): http://www.edmunds.com/about/press/cash-for-clunkers-results-finally-in-taxpayers-paid-24000-per-vehicle-sold-reports-edmundscom.html?articleid=159446&.

3. U.S. Department of Transportation, National Highway Traffic Safety Administration "Final Regulatory Impact Analysis," (July, 2009): http://www.nhtsa.gov/DOT/NHTSA/Rulemaking/Rules/Associated%20Files/CARS_FRIA.pdf.

4. Tami Luhby, "Obama Launches Mortgage Rescue Plan," CNNMoney. com, (April 16, 2009): http://money.cnn.com/2009/04/15/real_estate/ obama_mortgage_plan/index.htm. From CNNMoney, April 16, 2009 © 2009 Time Inc. Used under license. CNNMoney and Time Inc. are not affiliated with, and do not endorse products or services of, Licensee.

5. Les Christie, "Millions of Homeowners Eligible for Foreclosure Review," CNNMoney (November 1, 2011): http://money.cnn.com/2011/11/01/ real_estate/foreclosure_abuse/index.htm. From CNNMoney, November 1, 2011 © 2011 Time Inc. Used under license. CNNMoney and Time Inc. are not affiliated with, and do not endorse products or services of, Licensee.

Chapter Three

What Can American Politics Do for Me?

1. BBC News, "Greek Financial Crisis Explained," BBC Newsbeat (May 6, 2010): http://www.bbc.co.uk/newsbeat/10100201. Reprinted with permission.

2. Spyros Economides, "Viewpoint: The Politics of Greece's Financial Crisis," BBC News (June 17, 2011): http://www.bbc.co.uk/news/world-europe-13805391. Reprinted with permission.

3. Fiona Govan, "Spain Fears for Turning Back Clock on Liberal Reforms," *The Telegraph* (November 18, 2011): http://www.telegraph.co.uk/news/worldnews/europe/spain/8899630/Spain-fears-for-turning-back-clock-on-liberal-reforms.html.

4. Trading Economics, "Spain Unemployment Rate," (Accessed February 28, 2012): http://www.tradingeconomics.com/spain/indicators.

5. Nicole Winfield, "Berlusconi Resigns: Italian Prime Minister Silvio Berlusconi Steps Down After 17 Years," Associated Press (November 12, 2011): http://www.cbsnews.com/8301-202_162-57323652/italys-berlusconi-resigns-marking-end-of-era/. Used with permission of The Associated Press Copyright © 2012. All rights reserved.

6. Pew Forum on Religion & Public Life, "U.S. Religious Landscape Survey," (Accessed February 28, 2012): http://religions.pewforum.org/pdf/report-religious-landscape-study-appendix2.pdf.

7. *The Chicago Tribune,* "Obama's Energy Crisis," *The Chicago Tribune* (November 17, 2011): http://articles.chicagotribune.com/2011-11-17/news/ct-edit-solyndra-20111117_1_solyndra-loan-guarantee-renewable-energy. From *Chicago Tribune,* November 17, 2011 © 2011 *Chicago Tribune.* All rights reserved. Used by permission and protected by the Copyright Laws of the United States. The printing, copying, redistribution, or retransmission of this Content without express written permission is prohibited.

8. Matthew Mosk, "Energy Secretary Chu Takes Full Responsibility for Solyndra," ABC News (November 16, 2011): http://abcnews.

go.com/Blotter/energy-secretary-chu-takes-full-responsibility-solyndra/
story?id=14967189#.T3JYbNn0TMo.

9. *The Chicago Tribune,* "Obama's Energy Crisis."

10. OpenSecrets.org, "Barack Obama (D) Top Contributors," (Accessed February 28, 2012): http://www.opensecrets.org/pres08/contrib.
php?cid=N00009638.

11. Erika Lovley, "Obama Biggest Recipient of BP Cash," Politico (May 5, 2010): http://www.politico.com/news/stories/0510/36783.html. Reprinted with permission.

Chapter Four
Remove Corrupt Politicians from Office

1. Clea Benson and John McCormick, "Gingrich Said to be Paid About $1.6 Million by Freddie Mac," *Bloomberg News* (November 16, 2011): http://www.bloomberg.com/news/2011-11-16/gingrich-said-to-be-paid-at-least-1-6-million-by-freddie-mac.html.

2. Huff Post Politics, "Newt Gingrich Freddie Mac Fees: Former House Speaker Reportedly Received At Least $1.6 Million From Housing Giant," The Huffington Post (November 16, 2011): http://www.huffingtonpost.com/2011/11/16/newt-gingrich-freddie-mac_n_1096578.html.

3. John 12:24.

4. John 18:37.

5. John 18:38.

6. Daniel 1:3–6.

7. Daniel 1:8–10.

8. Daniel 1:12–17.

9. Daniel 1:18–20.

10. Daniel 2:10–19.

11. Ginnie Mae, "Media Center," (Accessed February 28, 2012): www.ginniemae.gov/media/ginnieFAQ.asp?Section=Media.

12. Eric Green, "Referendums Important for Letting Citizens Express Views," Mexidata (October 8, 2007): http://mexidata.info/id1559.html.

13. Jim Galloway, "Congress and a 16-Year Study of 'Insider Trading'" Political Insider (November 16, 2011): http://blogs.ajc.com/political-insider-jim-galloway/2011/11/16/congress-and-a-16-year-study-of-insider-trading/. Reprinted with permission.

14. Ida A. Brudnick, "Salaries of Members of Congress: A List of Payable Rates and Effective Dates, 1789–2008," Congressional Research Service (February 21, 2008): www.senate.gov/reference/resources/pdf/97-1011.pdf.

15. Ibid.

Chapter Five

A Mighty Army to Advance God's Kingdom

1. 1 Samuel 11:1–7.

2. 1 Samuel 11:10.

3. 1 Samuel 11:11.

4. Promise Keepers, "PK History—97 Stand in the Gap: a Sacred Assembly of Men," (Accessed February 28, 2012): http://www.promisekeepers.org/about/pk-history.

5. Scott Conroy and Shushannah Walshe, *Sarah from Alaska* (New York: PublicAffairs, 2009), 124. Copyright © 2010 Scott Conroy, Shushannah Walshe. Reprinted by permission of PublicAffairs, a member of the Perseus Books Group.

6. Ibid., 123–124.

7. Ibid.

8. Ibid.,140.

9. Sarah Palin, *Going Rogue, An American Life* (New York: HarperCollins Publishers, 2009), 277–278. Copyright © 2009 by Sarah Palin. All rights reserved. Reprinted by permission of HarperCollins Publishers.

10. Ibid.

11. Ibid., 272.

Chapter Six

Creating a Thriving Economy Without Government Stimulus

1. Karen Yourish and Laura Stanton, "Breaking Down Obama's Jobs Plan," *The Washington Post* (September 8, 2011): http://www.washingtonpost.com/business/economy/breaking-down-obamas-jobs-plan/2011/09/08/gIQAaZpEDK_graphic.html.

2. Tom Raum, "Small Dent in Jobless Rate Seen from Obama's Plan," The Associated Press (September 24, 2011): http://hamptonroads.com/2011/09/small-dent-jobless-rate-seen-obamas-plan.

3. Bradley Keoun and Phil Kuntz, "Wall Street Aristocracy Got $1.2 Trillion in Secret Loans," *Bloomberg News* (August 22, 2011): http://www.bloomberg.com/news/2011-08-21/wall-street-aristocracy-got-1-2-trillion-in-fed-s-secret-loans.html.

4. Edmund L. Andrews, "U.S. Adds Tariffs on Chinese Tires," *The New York Times* (September 11, 2009): http://www.nytimes.com/2009/09/12/business/global/12tires.html. From *The New York Times,* September 11, 2009 © 2009 *The New York Times*. All rights reserved. Used by permission and protected by the Copyright Laws of the United States. The printing, copying, redistribution, or retransmission of this Content without express written permission is prohibited.

Chapter Seven
Affordable Health Care Without Taxpayer-Funded Abortions

1. Darrell Issa, "Health Care Law Will Deepen Deficit," Politico (August 22, 2011): http://www.politico.com/news/stories/0811/61820.html. Reprinted with permission.

2. Mary Jo Layton and Lindy Washburn, "Aetna Sues Doctors Over Bills It Calls 'Excessive,'" *The Record* (March 25, 2011): http://www.northjersey.com/news/118635344_Aetna_sues_doctors_over_bills_it_calls__excessive_.html?c=y&page=1.

3. Most Reverend Michael J. Sheridan, "Dear Brothers and Sisters in Christ," Diocese of Colorado Springs letter dated February 1, 2012.

4. Douglas Johnson and Susan T. Muskett, "Senate-Passed Health Bill (H.R. 3590) Opens Door to Direct Federal Funding of Abortion Without Restriction in 1,250 Community Health Centers," National Right to Life Committee (March 18, 2010): http://www.nrlc.org/ahc/NRLCMemoCommHealth.html.

5. HR 3590, "Patient Protection and Affordable Care Act" p. 2356.

6. Robert A. Destro, "Abortion Coverage in the Senate Health Care Bill," The Catholic University of America (March 20, 2010): http://www.nrlc.org/AHC/DvSBA/Index.html and http://www.nrlc.org/AHC/DvSBA/ExhibitS-ProfessorDestroLetterOnCommunityHealthCenterProvisions.pdf.

7. Jeremiah 1:5.

8. Psalm 139:13 & 15–16.

9. Project Rachel Ministry, "Adverse Psychological Reactions: A Fact Sheet," (Accessed February 28, 2012): http://hopeafterabortion.com/?page_id=213#Literature.

10. National Right to Life, "The Presidential Record on Life," (Accessed February 28, 2012): http://www.nrlc.org/Records/bush43record0109.pdf and http://www.nrlc.org/Records/obamarecord.pdf.

Chapter Eight
Establishing Foreign Policy that Transforms the World

1. Transcript of President Bush's Speech to Joint Congress After the World Trade Center and Pentagon Bombings, "Justice Will Be Done," (September 20, 2001): http://www.greatdreams.com/bush_speech_92001.htm.

2. Daniel Trotta, "Cost of War at Least $3.7 Trillion and Counting," Reuters (June 29, 2011): http://www.reuters.com/article/2011/06/29/us-usa-war-idUSTRE75S25320110629. All rights reserved. Republication or redistribution of Thomson Reuters content, including by framing or similar means, is expressly prohibited without the prior written consent of Thomson Reuters. Thomson Reuters and its logo are registered trademarks or trademarks of the Thomson Reuters group of companies around the

world. © Thomson Reuters 2011. Thomson Reuters journalists are subject to an Editorial Handbook which requires fair presentation and disclosure of relevant interests.

3. Huang Jingjing, "Pakistan Angry at U.S. Bin Laden Raid," *Global Times* (May 7, 2011): http://world.globaltimes.cn/mid-east/2011-05/652521.html.

4. The Times of India, "Pakistan got $18 Billion Aid from U.S. Since 2001," *The Times of India* (February 23, 2010): http://articles.time-sofindia.indiatimes.com/2010-02-23/pakistan/28138643_1_civilian-aid-counterinsurgency-capability-fund-civilian-assistance.

5. United States Institute of Peace, "Priority Grant Competition," (Accessed February 28, 2012): http://www.usip.org/grants-fellowships/priority-grant-competition.

6. United States Institute of Peace, Education & Training, "Stabilization and Peacebuilding: Understanding Dynamic Processes and Making Them Work," (March 12–16, 2012): http://www.usip.org/education-training/courses/introduction-post-conflict-strategies-and-operations.

7. English meaning of the Holy Koran by Marmaduke Pickhall, Surah 58:22.

Chapter Nine

Outlawing Pornographic Images from the Public Domain

1. Rebecca Leung, "Porn in the U.S.A.," CBS News (December 5, 2007): http://www.cbsnews.com/stories/2003/11/21/60minutes/main585049.shtml. Reprinted with permission.

2. The United States Constitution, "Amendment 1—Freedom of Religion, Press, Expression," (Accessed February 28, 2012): http://www.usconstitution.net/const.html#Am1.

3. U.S. Constitution Online, "Constitutional Topic: The Constitution and Religion," (Accessed February 28, 2012): http://www.usconstitution.net/consttop_reli.html.

Chapter Ten

Upholding Our Nation's Ethics, Values and Morals

1. Devlin Barrett, "New Medical Marijuana Policy: Obama Administration Will Not Seek Arrests for People Following State Laws," Associated Press (October 19, 2009): http://www.huffingtonpost.com/2009/10/19/new-medical-marijuana-pol_n_325426.html. Used with permission of The Associated Press Copyright © 2012. All rights reserved.

2. Peter Nicholas, "Obama Assures He's Committed to Gay Rights," *The Los Angeles Times,* (June 30, 2009): http://articles.latimes.com/2009/jun/30/nation/na-obama-gays30. Copyright © 2009. Los Angeles Times. Reprinted with Permission.

3. Foon Rhee, "Obama Meets with Gay Leaders," *The Boston Globe* (June 29, 2009): http://www.boston.com/news/politics/politicalintelligence/2009/06/obama_meeting_w_1.html.

4. Ibid.

5. Jared Taylor, "Can It Happen Here? Sweden's 'Hate Speech' Laws Hateful—And Unequally Enforced," (October 2, 2004): http://www.vdare.com/articles/can-it-happen-here-swedens-hate-speech-laws-hateful-and-unequally-enforced.

6. LifeSiteNews.com, "Homosexual Hate Crime Signed into Law; Chilling Effect on Free Speech, Religion and Importing Material," (April 29, 2004): http://www.lifesitenews.com/news/archive/ldn/2004/apr/04042901.

7. Human Rights Commission, *Owens vs. Saskatchewan,* "Canadian Court Rules Bible Verses 'Hate Speech,'" (Accessed February 28, 2012): http://biblelight.net/bible-ruled-hate-speech.htm.

8. Ibid.

9. Ibid.

10. Ibid.

11. Jewish Publication Society's 1917 edition, "Leviticus Chapter 18," (Accessed February 28, 2012): http://www.mechon-mamre.org/e/et/et0318.htm.

12. Romans 1:26–32.

13. Catechism of the Catholic Church: 2357, Cf. *Gen* 19:1–29; *Rom* 1:24–27; *1 Cor* 6:10; *1 Tim* 1:10, CDF, *Persona humana* 8.

Appendix One

Our Founding Fathers' Religion

1. "Religious Affiliation of the Founding Fathers of the United States of America," (Accessed February 28, 2012): http://www.adherents.com/gov/Founding_Fathers_Religion.html.

Appendix Two

501(c)(3) Tax-Exempt Status

1. Internal Revenue Service, "Tax Guide for Churches and Religious Organizations," Publication 1828 (November 2009): www.irs.gov/pub/irs-pdf/p1828.pdf.

2. Ibid., 7.

3. Ibid., 12.

THE PRESIDENTIAL TEAM

If you would like to join the 2016 Christ-in-Congress Presidential Team, please consider submitting your résumé along with the online application form to:

www.CHRIST-IN-CONGRESS.com

Requirements for the Presidential Team are as follows:

1. Natural-born citizen of the United States
2. Between the ages of 40 to 55 years old
3. Financially independent/self-supported
4. Called by God and verified by our team's discernment
5. Willing to evangelize America for the next four years
6. Willing to travel/move to Washington, D.C.

COMING SOON

Once we have assembled our Presidential Team, we will publish their biographical information in a book entitled, *Hope for America, Meet the 2016 Presidential Team.*

HOPE FOR AMERICA

If you would like to participate in the
2016 Christ-in-Congress Campaign, please
consider distributing copies of *Hope for America*
to everybody you know. To purchase additional
copies of this book for evangelization purposes,
please use the following information:

Number of Copies	Price Each
1–5	$7.99
10–20	$6.75
30–50	$5.50
60–100	$4.25
200–1,000	$3.00

These prices include tax and shipping within the
United States. Thank you for your generous support.

Mail your payment to:

Valentine Publishing House
Hope for America — Christ-in-Congress
P.O. Box 27422
Denver, Colorado 80227